# HOPE FOR THE CITY

## TRANSFORMATIONAL
## LEADERSHIP
## DEVELOPMENT FOR
## URBAN MINISTRIES

*C. Anthony Hunt*

# HOPE FOR THE CITY:
## TRANSFORMATIONAL LEADERSHIP DEVELOPMENT FOR URBAN MINISTRIES

by C. Anthony Hunt

**Copyright 2022**

*The Rhodes-Fulbright Library series*

**ALL RIGHTS RESERVED.**

ISBN: 978-1-55605-534-8 Paperback

Ebook: 978-1-55605-535-5 E Book

# Contents

# *ACKNOWLEDGMENTS*

This volume has been written in the context of my village — my family, the church parishioners with whom I serve and lead as pastor, the academic institutions where I teach, and my students. I am forever grateful for my wife Lisa, and the life journey we continue to share. And I am grateful for our children — Marcus (deceased), Kristen, and Brian — and all I continue to learn through whom they are becoming. They continue to give me purpose and inspiration to be my best and give my very best to the church and world.

To Epworth Chapel United Methodist Church in Baltimore, Maryland, where I have had the privilege of serving as pastor for the past eleven years, and the Beloved Community Cooperative Ministry where I have also served as supervising pastor for the past three years, I am especially appreciative for the lessons we've learned as we've journeyed together in ministry. To the academic institutions where I am privileged to teach — St. Mary's Seminary and University in Baltimore, MD, Wesley Theological Seminary in Washington, DC, United Theological Seminary in Dayton, Ohio, and the Graduate Theological Foundation, Sarasota, Florida, and all of my students and faculty colleagues, I offer many thanks to you for continuing to stretch my thinking.

I dedicate this volume to my ancestors and my village. I stand on my ancestors' broad, strong, wise, and loving shoulders, and my village continues to be the wind beneath my wings. To God be the glory.

_C. Anthony Hunt_

# *INTRODUCTION*

*Also, seek the peace and prosperity of the city to which I have carried you into exile. Pray to the LORD for it, because if it prospers, you too will prosper. (Jeremiah 29:7)*

*"For I know the plans I have for you," declares the LORD, "plans to prosper you and not to harm you, plans to give you a future with hope." (Jeremiah 29:11)*

I am a native of Washington, DC born at Freedman's Hospital at Howard University where my father was a college student at the time of my birth, while my mother was attending another college in the city at the time. I was raised and educated in Southeast Washington, DC in a section of the city known as Anacostia, and in my teen years, my family moved to the Riggs Park community in Northeast Washington, DC. My early years shaped me and inculcated in me a love for the city – the richness of its life, culture, and diversity.

I attended college and seminary in urban settings in College Park, Maryland (the University of Maryland), Washington, DC (Wesley Theological Seminary), and Baltimore, Maryland (St. Mary's Seminary and University). For the majority of my years in ministry, I have served in urban contexts in Baltimore.

I remember first becoming aware of the complexities of city life as an elementary-school student in 1968, when on April 4th of that year, Rev. Dr. Martin Luther King, Jr. was assassinated in Memphis, Tennessee. I witnessed my hometown, Washington, DC erupt in the flames of protest in response to King's assassination. I witnessed members of the

Army National Guard move into my community for several days. Across the city, stores were looted and buildings and homes were destroyed.

As a young child, I remember being frightened by the rioting and the presence of Army National Guard troops as they traversed our neighborhood, just a few short blocks from our home. But I also remember having a sense of safety and security with my family and the community's ongoing protection and support. This experience, and the lasting image of crisis in our village in the aftermath of King's death, have served as the impetus for my passion for the city and urban ministry, and a commitment to helping improve conditions for urban churches and communities over the course of my ministerial career.

As a pastor, having served three churches in the greater Baltimore area, as a United Methodist district superintendent with administrative and missional leadership responsibilities with 88 Baltimore area churches (of the Baltimore-Harford and Baltimore Metropolitan United Methodist Districts), as a denominational executive resourcing urban congregations from Maine to West Virginia with the Multi-Ethnic Center for Ministry of the United Methodist Church, and as a teacher at three urban seminaries (Wesley Theological Seminary in DC, St. Mary's Seminary and University in Baltimore, and United Theological Seminary in Dayton, OH), I have had an opportunity to teach several academic courses in urban ministry, community engagement and leadership for those serving in urban ministry settings, led and designed several urban ministry convocations in Baltimore, and conducted numerous seminars, workshops, and consultations with churches, ministries, and nonprofit organizations in Baltimore,

Washington, DC, and in other cities across the United States and world.

My passion for leadership development and interest in the impact of effective, transformational leadership on organizational vitality, thriving, and growth dates back to my earlier formal education, having earned a Master of Business Administration degree, with a concentration in Management from Troy State University (AL), and advanced credentialing in management and leadership as a Certified Manager through the Institute of Certified Professional Managers at James Madison University (VA), along with completion of the Said Business School, University of Oxford's (UK) Executive Leadership Program, and the United State Army Officer Candidate School, Fort Benning, GA, among other military schools and leadership programs and courses.

From 2004-to 2012, I served as the United Methodist district superintendent in Baltimore. One day in 2007, the bishop called me into his office. As my direct supervisor, the bishop's question to me was, simply, *"Tony, what are we (you) going to do about Baltimore?"* That year, there were 278 people murdered in Baltimore. Those were 278 people whose loved ones – parents, spouses, children, and siblings were left to grieve.

The corollaries to the spiking murder rate in Baltimore in 2007 were ongoing increases in poverty rates in east, west, and south Baltimore, underachievement in most public schools, high rates of un- and under-employment, and high rates of drug and alcohol addiction. And the corollary to these community challenges was ongoing signs of decline among United Methodist churches across Baltimore as evidenced by declines in worship attendance, membership, community engagement, financial stability, and the closure of several congregations in the preceding ten years. And the bishop's question to me was a simple, but not so simple one – *"Tony, what are we (you) going to do about Baltimore?"*

As a result of the bishop's question to me, a strategic ministry plan for Baltimore emerged, which was embedded with a promise. With God's leading, we named the plan "Hope for the City", which was an initiative designed to strengthen churches and communities in Baltimore. The interesting thing about "Hope for the City" was that many people thought it unreasonable to claim that God had given us hope for Baltimore amid the apparently insurmountable challenges the city faced in 2007.

But, amidst apparent hopelessness, we are assured that God never leaves us with a predicament with no promise and hope. Jeremiah realized this, and God gave him a word to encourage the people. In the near hopeless situation in which Israel found themselves, Jeremiah said, *"seek the peace of the city where you find yourselves"* ... and then Jeremiah concluded with another word from the Lord, *"For I know the plans I have for you... plans to prosper you and not to harm you, plans to give you a future with hope" (Jeremiah 29:7, 11).*

Since 2011, I have served as the senior pastor of Epworth Chapel United Methodist Church in Baltimore, Maryland. Epworth Chapel was founded in 1956 in the, then, upper-middle-class suburban Lochearn community, and today is an urban congregation with more than 1200 members and more than 50 active ministries. Over its 66-year history, the church has gone through several demographic transitions. Today, Epworth Chapel is a multicultural, multi-national church, with members who were born in at least 15 different nations – mostly in Africa and the Caribbean.

Over the past eleven years, the church has experienced renewed vitality as evidenced by significant growth in worship attendance (an average of over 325 persons per week) and membership (over 200 new professing members have joined the church since 2011), expansion of program ministries, facility improvements (including the retirement of a $1 million capital debt in 2020), engagement in two major strategic planning processes (*Epworth 2020 and Epworth Dream 2030*), and organizational restructuring, with a focus on team-ministry.

During the COVID-19 pandemic (2020-22), Epworth Chapel, through its Mission, Outreach, and Faith in Action Team (MOFAT) and emergency food distribution center, in partnership with the Maryland Food Bank, was able to distribute over 300,000 pounds of food to members of the church and the broader community.

In 2020, Epworth Chapel completed a feasibility study to determine its strategic building and ministry needs and opportunities as the church moves into its next 66 years of ministry. A building project has begun and is projected to be a $4-5 million project. Identified opportunities for growth are in developing a sustainable model for identifying, nurturing, and developing transformational leadership and more fully connecting with the community surrounding the church.

For me, an ongoing question has been what are the best approaches to training and developing leaders to serve in urban ministry settings, especially for lay and clergy persons who may not attend seminary. This question is raised against the backdrop of the excellent ministry that many leaders and churches are already doing in urban contexts like Baltimore, and in light of leadership training that already exists. The next question is how to best apply learnings from biblical figures like Nehemiah and Paul who performed ministry in urban contexts and existing research and scholarship in transformational leadership to develop a comprehensive model for developing transformational leaders for effective service in urban ministry contexts.

This volume unites two of my academic and ministry interests and practices – transformational leadership and urban ministry. One of the clarion calls I have heard over the years is for leadership development and training that this specifically tailored to persons serving and leading in urban ministry contexts. This volume provides a framework that addresses this call and the need for a model for transformational leadership development for laity and clergy serving in urban ministry contexts. My prayer is that this volume will bless and serve as a resource for urban leaders, churches, and ministries in urban ministry contexts who are seeking to develop transformational leaders and develop vital churches and agencies that exist in urban areas.

# CHAPTER ONE
## GOD AND THE CITY:
## BIBLICAL AND THEOLOGICAL
## PERSPECTIVES

*"God is in the midst of the city; it shall not be moved; God will help it when the morning dawns." (Psalm 46:5)*

Benjamin Tonna points out that almost in line with contemporary urbanization, the Scriptures begin in a garden and end in a city. To better understand the role of the city in God's plan, one has the biblical vision of the New Jerusalem — the renewed city — in the Book of Revelation (Rev. 21:2).[1] This vision seems to indicate the direction in which the progressive activation of God's plan of salvation moves and points out the stages needed for its development. In this light, the reality of the contemporary city takes on another aspect, opening itself to new horizons and – ultimately — salvation.[2]

God's work of salvation has been and continues to be needed in cities. Phillip Reed asserts that if the church is going to adequately address the needs of the community, then it will need to recover the biblical concept of salvation. In the Old Testament, salvation meant primarily deliverance from one's

---

[1] Benjamin Tonna, *Gospel for the Cities: A Socio-Theology of Urban Ministry,* (Maryknoll, NY: Orbis Books, 1985), 121.

[2] Tonna, *Gospel for the Cities*, 121.

enemies or danger.[3] Salvation was often a community event. The major event in the life of Israel, which contained God's salvation for God's people, was the deliverance of the people from Egypt. In the New Testament, the concept of salvation took on a wider meaning, which included first and foremost the forgiveness of sins through Jesus Christ, but which also included the concepts of salvation from poverty and destruction included in the Old Testament.[4]

According to Robert Carle and Louis DeCaro, cities have existed for over 10,000 years as a form of social organization. In biblical times, Jericho grew from a village to a city of about 3000 in 7000 BCE. In 3500-4000 BCE, the first large cities (25,000 people) were established in Mesopotamia. The word city appears 1090 times in the Old Testament and over 160 times in the New Testament. At least 133 different cities are noted by name in the Bible.[5]

The Scriptures also contain dozens of references to urban characters who put flesh, bones, and life on biblical ministry models. Thirteen chapters of Genesis, for example, focus on an economic developer named Joseph, who developed, for a pagan pharaoh, two seven-year plans, one for budget deficits and one for budget surpluses. Nehemiah, the general contractor and two-term governor of Jerusalem made many deals with state officials to rebuild the walls of his ruined city.[6]

---

[3] Phillip Reed, "Toward a Theology of Christian Community Development," in John M. Perkins, *Restoring At-Risk Communities: Doing it Right and Doing it Together* (Grand Rapids, MI: Baker Books, 1995), 38.
[4] Reed, "Toward a Theology of Christian Community Development", 38.
[5] Robert D. Carle and Louis A. DeCaro, Jr., eds. *Signs of Hope in the City: Ministries of Community Renewal* (Valley Forge, PA: Judson Press, 1999), 5.
[6] Carle and DeCaro, *Signs of Hope in the City*, 5.

Ray Bakke and Jim Hart assert that Paul's work in the early church was entirely urban, centered in Antioch, Ephesus, Corinth, Jerusalem, and Rome.[7] The Gospel was spread from city to city as Paul preached and the message spread to Asia, Africa, and Europe. Many of Paul's epistles are addressed to cities — including Rome, Corinth, Thessalonica, Galatia, Ephesus, Philippi, and Colossi. Paul wrote these letters to persons in cities within the context of the real theological, ethical and communal issues they were facing in trying to live out their new faith in Christ in urban contexts. It is interesting to note that Paul addressed issues such as marriage, divorce, poverty, sharing of resources, unemployment, economic development, health concerns, the need to work cooperatively, and many others similar to those faced by persons and churches in cities today.

Tonna believes that as a symbol of God's sacred place and God's divine activity, the early cities' basic weakness (as exemplified by Babylon) seems to have been the incapacity to maintain communication among human beings — leading to detachment, alienation, and isolation. This incapacity is related to several inherent human needs — (1) the need for community — our inherent need to move toward "common unity"; (2) the need to establish justice and order in the land; (3) the need for communion, the search for the sacred in the city, and ways to sacramentally and symbolically bring forth a sense of the unity of persons in God amidst the human diversity that encompasses the city; and (4) the need for solidarity and the development of

---

[7] Ray Bakke and Jim Hart, *The Urban Christian: Effective Ministry in Today's Urban World* (Downers Grove, IL: InterVarsity Press, 1987), 80.

a means of redefining the structures of life.[8] Tonna suggests that God responds to these human needs with a new creative act, the act of salvation. This is the hope of the city. Salvation is thus to be viewed as an individual and communal prospect.[9]

Because many of God's people have historically resided in urban areas, this is the place where God's activity and saving grace can often be manifest in its most profound, pronounced, and powerful ways. The New City is presented as the definitive context for the reconciliation of humanity with God. It becomes the ultimate point of the impulse that has long moved humanity, now that God, in Christ, is already definitively present among human beings and accepted by them. Jerusalem is thus the completion of the history of the city. In the Book of Revelation, there is another city, Babylon, and John is doubtless thinking also of Bethel, a symbol of the creative powers of humanity.[10]

Babylon, like present-day cities, had its strengths and weaknesses. Ronald Peters proposes that the image of Babylon as the "Bad City" has, in large measure, become the paradigm for understanding the city in general. According to Peters, it is a paradigm of moral dysfunction, injustice, violence, and oppression — where people are in the city because they have been displaced from where they want to be (Jerusalem). The potential of the "Good City" embodies relationship-building as a part of its ministry. Urban ministers then become the embodiment of reconciliation, compassion, and justice.[11]

Cities as God's sacred places where large populations of God's people have resided have been the places where the

---

[8] Tonna, *Gospel for the Cities*, 128-130.

[9] Tonna, *Gospel for the Cities*, 130-132.

[10] Tonna, *Gospel for the Cities*, 132.

[11] Peters, *Urban Ministry*, 16.

earliest civilized cultures gathered and developed. These are the places where the earliest codified laws have been found. It was in these first cities that agrarian economies, governments and administration, and science began to develop. In these lands can also be found the roots of Judeo-Christian thought and culture.[12]

Cities have also been places where diversity among people converges — socially, economically, politically, racially, and religiously. The word that Jesus used in the marching orders for his church is the Greek word *ethnos*, from which the word "ethnic" is derived.

According to Phillip Reed, it is important to understand the message of salvation for the inner city with the call that Jesus gave to his church in the Great Commission: "Then Jesus came to them and said:

> All authority in heaven and on earth has been given to me. Therefore, go and make disciples of all nations, baptizing them in the name of the Father and of the Son and the Holy Spirit, and teaching them to obey everything I have commanded you. And surely, I am with you always, to the very end of the age (Matt. 28:18-20).[13]

According to Bryan Stone and Claire Wolfteich, for many Christians, the city is one of the last places to come to mind when thinking about where we encounter God in our lives and find spiritual renewal.[14] But though the city is a place of

---

[12] Tonna, *Gospel for the Cities*, 121.

[13] Reed, "Toward a Theology of Christian Community Development," 38-39.

[14] Bryan Stone and Claire Wolfteich, *Sabbath in the City: Sustaining Pastoral Excellence* (Louisville: Westminster John Knox Press, 2008), 77.

distraction, busyness, and frenzied activity and though it is often imagined in Scripture as a place of unrest, idolatry, and wickedness, it is also the holy habitation of God; as the psalmist says, *"God is in the midst of the city; it shall not be moved; God will help it when the morning dawns"* (Psalm 46:5).[15]

Indeed, from biblical antiquity, God has been and continues to be present in cities among the people and processes that exist in urban areas. And the promise for cities into the future is that the prophet Jeremiah's words are still pertinent as the Lord said in Jeremiah 29:11, *"For I know the plans I have for you...plans to prosper you and not to harm you, plans to give you a future with hope."*

---

[15] Stone and Wolfteich, *Sabbath in the City,* 78.

# CHAPTER TWO
## LIVING FOR THE CITY, PART I:
## PERSPECTIVES ON THE URBAN CONTEXT
## AND URBANIZATION

> *It is important that different parts of the city be well integrated and that those who live there have a sense of the whole, rather than being confined to one neighborhood and failing to see the larger city as a space that they share with others.*
> *Pope Francis (Laudat Si)[16]*

In *The Evolution of the American Society*, Howard Chudacoff and Judith Smith trace the history and evolution of cities and urban areas from the 17th through the 20th century. They point out that the history of city-building on the North American continent preceded the arrival of the Europeans.[17] Before 1800, only 3 percent of the world's population lived in towns of more than 5,000 inhabitants. Chudacoff and Smith point to recent phenomena in American cities such as the decline of many central cities, the revival of other central cities, the hope of educational and economic opportunity, the realities of drugs and homelessness, the rise of Sun Belt cities, and the decline of Frost Belt cities as some of the key indicators that characterize cities today.[18]

---

[16] Pope Francis, *Laudato Si – Encyclical Letter* (Vatican City: Liberia Elditrice Vaticana, June 18, 2015), 151.

[17] Howard Chudacoff and Judith Smith, *The Evolution of the American Society* (Englewood Cliffs, NJ: Prentice Hall, 1988), 1.

[18] Chudacoff and Smith, *The Evolution of the American Society,* 294-308.

The growing predominance of cities in America and around the world is identified as the process of urbanization. Regarding urbanization, Harvey Cox states:

> In trying to define the term urbanization... we are confronted with the fact that social scientists are not entirely agreed on what it means. It is clear, however, that urbanization is not a quantitative term. It does not refer to population size or density, geographic extent, or a particular form of government. Admittedly some of the character of modern urban life would not be possible without giant populations concentrated on enormous contiguous landmasses. But urbanization is not something that refers only to the city.[19]

According to Ronald Peters, urbanization is typically understood as the process of interlocking social, cultural, economic, political, religious, and spatial characteristics that reflect the environment and ethos of the city.[20] Benjamin Tonna defines the process of urbanization as the phenomenon by which millions of people move en masse from rural to metropolitan areas — and more importantly — which transforms their lifestyle.[21]

Urbanization and rapid growth of cities in the United States in the 19th and into the 20th century were associated with industrialization, which resulted in an influx of immigrants and

---

[19] Harvey Cox, *The Secular City: Secularization and Urbanization in Theological Perspective* (New York: MacMillan, 1966), 3-4.

[20] Peters, *Urban Ministry*, 26.

[21] Tonna, *Gospel for the Cities*, 5.

migrants to provide labor for emerging factories. As society became more sophisticated in the growing and distribution of food, labor needs for farming were lessened. The development of the factory system led to a concentration of labor and services in urban areas.[22]

Urbanization is a complex, continuous process. It is both the movement of people from rural to urban areas and the spread of urban cultural patterns to rural areas (which over time become more urban in character). According to Peters, the urbanization of the world and the closely related issues of ministry in urbanized contexts, are much more involved than mere statistics about population shifts or other demographic profiles. It is a subject essentially concerned with human relationships and divine realities as these are experienced in the ecology of the social, spatial, and spiritual context we refer to as the urban environment and what the urban area reveals to us about God.[23]

Urbanization is a global phenomenon. In recent decades, the world has experienced unprecedented urban growth with most of the growth occurring in less developed countries. In 1975 — 37 percent of the world's population lived in urban areas; in 2000 - 47 percent lived in urban areas; in 2015 — over 60 percent of the world's population lived in urban areas, and by 2030 — it is projected that over 80 percent of the world's population will live in urban areas. In the U.S. — 75% of the population lives in urban areas, and half of the population lives in 38 metropolitan centers (Standard Metropolitan Statistical Areas).[24]

---

[22] Tonna, *Gospel for the Cities,* 5.

[23] Peters, *Urban Ministry*, 8.

[24] Peters, *Urban Ministry*, 7.

21

David Claerbaut asserts that urbanization is an irreversible trend. At the beginning of the 20th century, about 8 percent of the world's population lived in cities. By the early 1980s, half of the world's population resided in urban areas. Demographics project that almost all of the world's population growth over the next thirty years will be in urban areas.[25]

According to Peters, the realities that define contexts in which urban ministry is carried out today can be summed up in three words — alienation, fear, and violence.[26] He asserts that alienation, fear, and violence in urban contexts are relational manifestations of the far deeper issue pondered throughout the history of human theological reflection: the problem of evil.[27] Consequently, evil is malevolent, deceptive, and destructive. It is contagious. Evil warps the spiritual perception, distorts material vision, and dulls the ethical senses in a manner that often belies its sinister and ultimately fatal qualities.[28]

Several factors contribute to challenges that exist in many urban areas. According to William Julius Wilson, while structural forces are the primary cause of inner-city poverty and other social disparities among Blacks, it is necessary to also examine cultural forces that have emerged, over time, due to the structural forces.[29] He states that two types of social forces contribute directly to racial group outcomes such as differences in poverty and employment rate: social acts and social

---

[25] David Claerbaut, *Urban Ministry in a New Millennium* (Federal Way, WA: World Vision, 2005), 1.

[26] Peters, *Urban Ministry,* 8.

[27] Peters, *Urban Ministry,* 8.

[28] Peters, *Urban Ministry,* 13.

[29] William Julius Wilson, *More than Just Race: Being Black and Poor in the Inner City* (New York: W. W. Norton, 2009), 3.

processes. *Social acts* refer to the behavior of individuals within a society. Examples of social acts are stereotyping, stigmatization, and discrimination in hiring. *Social processes* refer to the "machinery" of society that exists to promote ongoing relations among members of the larger group. Examples of social processes that contribute directly to racial group outcomes include laws, policies, and institutional practices that exclude people based on their race or ethnicity.[30]

Numerous challenges confront the future of cities and their vitality. According to Charles Euchner and Stephen McGovern, these challenges include poverty, economic development, housing, education, and crime.[31] They propose a communitarian approach aimed at bridging longstanding divisions and assert that anyone who wants to do something about the "urban crisis" needs to acknowledge political, social, and economic constraints. But it is also important to avoid paralysis. Within these constraints, people have the opportunity to make their own politics. Even modest urban revitalization policies at the outset can begin to inspire civic engagement, which can foster the development of a new political culture that respects community, participation in public life, and a more active role for government in promoting opportunity.[32]

Baltimore, MD is a case in point of a city where these challenges have been precipitous over time. Lawrence Brown, a former associate professor at Morgan State University, argues that in Baltimore, there have been over 100 years of patterns of

---

[30] Wilson, *More than Just Race*, 5.

[31] Charles Euchner and Stephen McGovern, *Urban Policy Reconsidered: Dialogues on the Problems and Prospects of American Cities* (New York: Routledge, 2003), 2-33.

[32] Euchner and McGovern, *Urban Policy Reconsidered*, 32-33.

racial segregation, and practices and policies that promoted the exploitation of black residents.[33] Investment in Baltimore is fragmented by race, income, and geography, creating what he finds to be the socio-political phenomenon of "two Baltimores" as imaged in "the white L vs. the black Butterfly". The geographical shape of an 'L' in predominantly white communities gives these communities more resources and support, and the shape of a 'Butterfly' spans the east and west sides of the city in predominantly black communities, which are more likely to be neglected.[34] Brown asserts that as a result of these patterns and practices, Baltimore is a city that is hyper-segregated into two parts and that the city's hyper-segregated neighborhoods experience radically different realities. Due to these dynamics, white neighborhoods form the shape of a geographic 'L' running through the center of the city, and accumulate structural advantages, while black neighborhoods, shaped in the form of a butterfly, on the city's east and west, accumulate structural disadvantages. Baltimore's hyper-segregation is the root cause of racial inequity, poverty, health inequities/disparities, addiction, educational inequality, and community unrest and violence.[35]

Bryan Stone and Claire Wolfteich similarly identify six critical challenges in cities that can serve to affect the sustenance of ministry leadership excellence in urban communities. These challenges are (1) transitions occurring in declining neighborhoods, commuting neighborhoods, and aging congregations; (2) the expansive nature of social need,

---

[33] Lawrence Brown, "Two Baltimore's: The White L vs. the Black Butterfly," *Baltimore Sun,* June 28, 2016.

[34] Lionel Foster, "The Black Butterfly: Racial Segregation and Investment Patterns in Baltimore," in  Urban Institute, February 5, 2019.

[35]  Brown, "Two Baltimores: The White L vs. the Black Butterfly".

where churches are key places where people continue to go to seek help; (3) local church identity in the context of denominational bodies which often challenge churches' relevance in local communities; (4) diversity and immigration, and questions of how churches effectively address the needs of the young, elderly, economically and socially diverse; (5) division and alienation among diverse groups of people within communities; and (6) the lack of resources, and thus the need to devise needs-based and asset-based strategies and approaches to addressing the scarcity of resources.[36]

Stone and Wolfteich assert that the keys to sustaining leadership excellence in urban ministry settings include: (1) Cultivating holy friendships; (2) Sabbath practices that honor creation and promote liberation; (3) Renewing the spirit; and (4) Finding God in the city.[37] Urban leaders need to seek and sustain an "urban spirituality" that is attuned to discovering and creating necessary rhythms, patterns, and practices to nourish the leader's spirit.[38]

In *Crisis in the Village: Restoring Hope in African American Communities,* Robert Franklin offers a sociological analysis of various challenges that exist in urban contexts, and by extension, that confront many of those serving in urban ministry settings, and what he refers to as "crisis in the village".[39] For Franklin, the challenges facing many urban communities today are contradictory to the very nature of the

---

[36] Stone and Wolfteich, *Sabbath in the City,* 1-20.

[37] Stone and Wolfteich, *Sabbath in the City,* 26-90.

[38] Stone and Wolfteich, *Sabbath in the City*, xvii.

[39] Robert M. Franklin, *Crisis in the Village: Restoring Hope in African American Communities* (Minneapolis, MN: Fortress Press, 2007), 1-40.

foundations upon which these communities have historically been shaped.

Franklin, himself a product of the South-side of Chicago near the Robert Taylor Homes, which before its demolition was the largest public housing project in the world, points out that much of the demise and crisis in the proverbial village today is rooted in factors like rising levels of unemployment and underemployment, the lack of affordable housing, and a crisis in urban healthcare. These root causes and their results, including rising dropout rates among students in urban school systems and rising levels of youth violence, present significant challenges to the prospect of the realization of a *restored hope* in urban communities across our nation.[40]

Franklin asserts that for restoration to occur in urban communities, collaboration is essential. His collaborative approach to "restoring the village" has six interrelated aspects: (1) focused conversation, (2) collaborative leadership, (3) vision and planning, (4) accountability and action, (5) sustaining and fundraising, and (6) documenting and celebrating progress.[41]

The conditions in many cities today point to the dynamic and dialectical forces and factors of tremendous need and opportunity, apparent despair, and hope. As cities are centers of life and activity and will become even more so in the future, they will serve as places of key indicators of how society as a whole will flourish.

In summary, several unique dynamics, challenges, and opportunities are entailed in urban contexts, and by extension -

---

[40] Franklin, *Crisis in the Village*, 1-40.
[41] Franklin, *Crisis in the Village*, 227-244.

urban ministry contexts. These dynamics, challenges, and opportunities call for leadership that fits the particular needs and opportunities of ministry contexts. Cases of effective urban ministry leaders like Rudy Rasmus at St. John's United Methodist Church in Houston, TX, Mark Gornik at New Song Church in Baltimore, MD, and Roger Gench at New York Avenue Presbyterian Church in Washington, DC will be discussed in this volume, and point to the importance of transformational leadership and qualities like relationality, collaboration, and persistence as being essential to developing people, building urban ministries, and impacting communities.

# CHAPTER THREE
## LIVING FOR THE CITY, PART II:
## PERSPECTIVES ON URBAN MINISTRY

*Being a caring and considerate presence can help build trust and form community.*
**Leah Gunning Francis (Ferguson and Faith)**

Ministry in urban contexts presents unique challenges, one of which is developing effective leaders who are equipped to lead persons, churches, and other community organizations toward effectiveness, vitality, and growth. According to David Claerbaut, a good working definition of urban ministry is that it is a community, usually organized formally, of God's people in the city. Ministry is carried out both within, to the members, and without, to the world.[42] Ronald Peters defines urban ministry as a way of understanding God, based on the dynamics of the city, and involves a theological praxis that seeks to enhance the quality of life for all creation.[43]

In characterizing urban ministry, Robert Franklin details five types of ministry engagement in urban contexts.[44] These five types are (1) *Ministries of Charity and Mercy* that provide direct relief to people who suffer. Most churches

---

[42] Claerbaut, *Urban Ministry in a New Millennium*, x.

[43] Peters, *Urban Ministry,* 8.

[44] Robert M. Franklin, see preface to eds. Eldin Villafane, Bruce Jackson, Robert Evans, Alice Frazier, *Transforming the City: Reframing Education for Urban Ministry* (Grand Rapids, MI: Eerdmans, 2001), xxii.

participate in some form of this type of ministry. (2) *Ministries of Nurture* that offer sustained support to assist people in becoming self-reliant. This demands a greater commitment of time and resources than ministries of charity and mercy. (3) *Ministries that provide Human Services* that reflect the way the church structures itself (often through the creation of private, nonprofit organizations, e.g. 501c3 and community development corporations) to provide services such as child care, job training, community services, etc. (4) *Ministries of Justice* that provide a prophetic, public witness of social activism. In this way, the church becomes a voice for the voiceless and a forum for the powerless. (5) *Ministries of Comprehensive Community Transformation* that involve developing and announcing a vision of the "good community". Churches engaged in such ministries take a leading role in acquiring vacant land, organizing capital, incubating micro-enterprises, and directing public and private resources.

According to Mark Gornik, the goal of urban mission or community ministry is not to obtain power or influence, nor can ever be to 'take over' the neighborhood. Rather, the church's goal is to be God's peace in the broken places and bear witness to the kingdom of God.[45]

Franklin asserts that leaders who engage the city in these and many other ways must be formed and nurtured. Transformed nonconformists do not appear automatically or accidentally.[46] At best, such leaders emerge from learning contexts that have been forged in the flame of experimentation, evaluation, prayer, and practical, critical, and theological thinking. Strategic theological thinking and planning about

---

[45] Gornik, *To Live in Peace*, 124.
[46] Franklin, in *Transforming the City*, xxiii.

urban ministry should give some attention to matters of curriculum, faculty, institutional partnership, evaluation, and the warrants (biblical, theological, and ethical) for such ministry.[47]

Peters asserts that there are eight interwoven areas of urban ministry upon which churches should focus. These areas are (1) Economic Life, (2) Educational Systems, (3) Family Life, (4) Public Health, (5) Ethnic/Racial Relations, (6) Religious Culture, (7) Restorative Justice (Civil/Political Rights), and (8) Environment (Environmental Justice).[48] These eight areas – what Peters refers to as lenses and focus areas in urban ministry - represent themes that characterize the context of urban ministry. These focus areas relate to public issues that tend to characterize urban ministry globally in all regions and cultures and comprise organizational networks common to urban areas around the world.[49]

He further asserts that one of the biggest challenges facing practitioners of urban ministry has less to do with the geographical and sociological context of the city itself than with pervasive realities that define the era in which we live.[50] Peters proposes that several chasms exist in cities that serve as points of division and alienation, and point to the need for reconciliation. He characterizes a chasm as a deep cleft of depression, a gorge, that constitutes a division in an otherwise relatively unbroken stretch of landscape and, as such, symbolizes much that characterizes urban ministry.[51]

---

[47] Franklin, in *Transforming the City,* xxiii.
[48] Peters, *Urban Ministry,* 159-165.
[49] Peters, *Urban Ministry,* 159-165.
[50] Peters, *Urban Ministry,* 11-18.
[51] Peters, *Urban Ministry,* 19.

He asserts that at least four chasms must be bridged in developing an approach to doing urban ministry: (1) *The urban ministry and Christian ministry chasm*, which is an artificial barrier that must be removed. (2) *The urban and rural chasm* where there's a failure to see the fundamental unity that exists between urban and rural communities. Many of the challenges that exist in urban communities also exist in rural communities. (3) *The ethics and evangelism chasm* where there needs to be a recognition of urban ministry's roots in justice advocacy (ethical agency) and evangelistic mission (speaking the Gospel). (4) *The urban as a code word and urban as a theological symbol chasm* where "urban" is often a code word for "Black", "Brown", "those people", "poor'', and "non-mainstream''. Peters asserts that as a theological symbol – urban is an eschatological paradigm and symbol of hope.[52]

The ministry of Jesus was one of reconciliation, for God was in Christ, reconciling the world with Godself" (II Cor. 5:19). Christ left the church with the commission to go and do likewise. The church is the vehicle that continuously carries out the ministry of God in the world. The ministry of the church, through its various ways of serving the world, is the bridge between God and humanity; it is God working in and through persons as God continues to reconcile the world with Godself.

Dietrich Bonhoeffer characterized the church as Christ existing as community. He explicated several characteristics of Christian community (the church). First, he saw a relationship between Christian community and sanctification. He stated, "Christian community is like the *Christian's sanctification*. It is a gift of God that we cannot claim. Only God knows the real state of our fellowship or our sanctification. What may appear

---

[52] Peters, *Urban Ministry*, 20-26.

to be weak and trifling to us may be great and glorious to God."[53]

Second, Bonhoeffer pointed to *Christ and the Holy Spirit as the foundations of Christian community.* He stated, "Because Christian community is founded solely on Jesus Christ, it is a spiritual and not a psychic reality. In this, it differs absolutely from all other communities... The community of the Spirit is the fellowship of those who are called by Christ; the human community of spirit is the fellowship of devout souls."[54]

Third, according to Bonhoeffer, *Christian community is marked by spiritual love.* Because spiritual love does not desire but rather serves, it loves the enemy as a brother (or sister). It originates neither in the brother (or sister) nor in the enemy but in Christ and the Word. Humanity's love can never understand spiritual love, for spiritual love is from above; it is something completely strange, new, and incomprehensible to all earthly love.[55]

Ministry, then, is to be understood as an act of compassion and love and grows out of God's gracious love for humanity. It is how salvation in Christ is offered to the world. This understanding of ministry is perhaps most clearly demonstrated in the way that Jesus called, taught, and then sent those who would accept his teachings and be in ministry with the world (*missio Dei*).

Roger Gench, in *Theology from the Trenches: Reflections on Urban Ministry,* offers a covenantal model for doing urban ministry and characterizes urban ministry as a

---

[53] Dietrich Bonhoeffer, *Life Together: The Classic Exploration of Faith in Community.* trans. John Doberstein (New York: Harper Collins, 1954), 30.
[54] Bonhoeffer, *Life Together,* 31.
[55] Bonhoeffer, *Life Together,* 35.

covenant community where it is shaped through establishing the cruciform covenant, creating a covenant community, engaging a covenant community, and deepening a covenant community.[56]

Gench provides a theoretical and practical framework for how organizing ministry for transformation and growth might occur through developing a covenant community and asserts that urban congregations committed to ministry in their contexts grapple with formidable issues endemic to these contexts – homelessness, scarcity of living wage jobs, racism, mental illness, crime, education and economic disparities. According to Gench, the covenant began/begins with the redeeming/saving work of Christ on the Cross.[57]

God's culminating vision in the Bible is an urban one – a vision of the New Heaven and New Earth, the holy city, the New Jerusalem, coming down of heaven from God (Rev. 21:2).[58] Cruciformity and crucifixion are (1) historical reality, and (2) a symbol of the abuse of power. The crucifixion is symbolic of any exercise of power that dominates, deforms, or defaces human life.[59]

Gench then offers perspectives on how to effectively organize for congregational renewal in urban contexts. He draws on Mike Gecan's four tools for effective organizing and analyzing one's congregation and community.[60] These tools are (1) The individual (relational) meeting; (2) Power analysis of

---

[56] Roger J. Gench, *Theology from the Trenches: Reflections on Urban Ministry* (Louisville: Westminster John Knox Press, 2014), 29-77.
[57] Gench, *Theology from the Trenches*, 3.
[58] Gench, *Theology from the Trenches*, 4.
[59] Gench, *Theology from the Trenches*, 5.
[60] Gench, *Theology from the Trenches*, 25.

both the church and organizations in the community; (3) Teaching and training; and (4) Action and evaluation.

In terms of creating a covenant community as a framework for community organizing, Gench observes that in the Gospel of Luke, Jesus was always eating, and always going to/from a meal, and proposes that one-on-one meetings are a foundational aspect of creating a covenant community. The focus of these relational meetings should be on building relationships and creating a covenantal culture of deep and abiding connection through the hearing and telling of stories.[61]

Gench offers that the next step is engaging the covenant community. This entails involving the community in a listening campaign. He states that "Listening is at the heart of communal life" as listening facilitates collective discernment and is a means by which people can be integrated and engaged in the shared ministry of the church. Engaging the covenant community essentially involves living into the Great Commandment, which calls for the integration of heart, mind, and will as an embodiment of God's love.[62]

According to Gench, the final step in organizing a church/community for action and change is deepening the covenant community. This is an ongoing process that occurs through contemplation and entails both personal and corporate prayer and worship, and creates the space in which persons discern a yearning for God and God's people.[63]

In *Walking with Nehemiah,* Joseph Daniels utilizes the biblical image of Nehemiah walking and surveying the walls of Jerusalem, which lie in ruins as the starting point for the

---

[61] Gench, *Theology from the Trenches,* 29-44.
[62] Gench, *Theology from the Trenches,* 45-62.
[63] Gench, *Theology from the Trenches,* 63-78.

transformation of faith leaders, the church, and the community. Daniels is the pastor of Emory Fellowship United Methodist Church in Washington, DC, an urban congregation that has grown from 25 active members in 1992 to now over 1,000 members. He asserts that leaders must survey the pockets of their churches and communities that are in ruin and then respond accordingly. "It isn't until you know for whom or what your heart breaks that God can reveal where in the community and with whom your ministry needs to be done."[64] When we get to the place where we can replace statistics with faces and real life-stories then we will be more inclined to help and less apt to hinder or simply hide.[65]

Daniels recommends that leaders engage in "Nehemiah Walks" of their communities, and suggests that several things are important to ensure that the "Nehemiah Walk" yields clarity for what is needed for the restoration of the community. First and foremost, he shares that "Relational 1:1" campaigns inside the congregation are an effective way of discovering the heartbreak of the congregation."[66] Relational 1:1s can be an informative and helpful tool for understanding what issues are important to the life of the church and community members, and where change is occurring inside the church walls, and in the community.

A major portion of the work of transformation is recognizing that everybody doesn't always get on board. Daniels states:

---

[64] Joseph Daniels, *Walking with Nehemiah: Your Community is Your Congregation* (Nashville: Abingdon Press), 1.
[65] Daniels, *Walking with Nehemiah,* 1.
[66] Daniels, *Walking with Nehemiah.* 14.

The leaders of the congregation have to acknowledge that the congregation is not all-in about God's restoration process. The congregation has to decide whether it is going to play church or be the church. Usually, at this stage, church councils or leadership teams have to have a "come to Jesus" meeting about what the congregation is about and what the congregation is going to be known for.[67]

In *Restoring At-risk Communities*, John Perkins asserts that urban ministry starts with identifying the needs of the people. Responding to those needs in holistic ways is based on Biblical principles, is tested by time, develops and utilizes leaders in the community, encourages relocation to live among the people, demands reconciliation, and empowers through redistribution of all community members by sharing skills, talents, education, and resources.[68] He suggests that we must practice the "felt need" concept of engaging members of at-risk communities by "starting with people's felt needs".[69]

Perkins offers critical insights on approaches to restoring challenged urban communities through what he identifies as the 3-Rs — Reconciliation, Relocation, and Redistribution.[70] He offers the three-step journey (admit, submit, and commit) as a tool for racial, economic, and social

[67] Daniels, *Walking with Nehemiah,* 38.
[68] John Perkins, *Restoring At-Risk Communities: Doing it Together and Doing it Right* (Grand Rapids, MI: Baker Books, 1995), 26.
[69] Perkins, *Restoring At-Risk Communities*, 17.
[70] Perkins, *Restoring At-Risk Communities,* 75-162.

reconciliation, where separation and distance exist among people.

First, he writes of the positive effects of the physical *relocation* of people into the communities in which they are doing ministry as a means of building trust and relationships and demonstrating signs of full investment in the well-being of communities. He points out that Jesus lived among the people he served during his earthly ministry.

Then, Perkins discusses the importance of people's *reconciliation* with God and their neighbor.[71] Reconciliation gets to the crux of community connection and engagement in urban ministry contexts. It requires a decisive paradigm shift — one evidenced by friendships of trust, common mission, and mutual submission that go beyond Sunday morning.[72]

Finally, Perkins discusses the importance of *redistribution*.[73] His thesis is that while economic redistribution is important in ministering in many urban communities, the most important things to be redistributed are people in the community. Justice cannot be achieved from a distance. Redistribution results when people, reconciled with God and each other, share whatever resources they have to work together for the common good of the community.

Several best practices can be identified for effective urban ministry. Jason Byassee, in "Strategies for Urban Ministry", offers case studies of several churches in Chicago that have sought to address the challenges facing their churches and communities through ways of improvising, trying new

---

[71] Perkins, *Restoring At-Risk Communities,* 75-106.
[72] Perkins, *Restoring At-Risk Communities,* 110.
[73] Perkins, *Restoring At-Risk Communities,* 139-159.

approaches, and risking failure.[74] His findings are that successful urban ministries focus on doing a few things well, like connecting with people through hospitality, art, companionship, theater, food, or service.

In terms of leadership traits that are important for persons serving in urban contexts, Nile Harper, in *Urban Churches: Vital Signs - Beyond Charity Toward Justice*, identifies 15 "vital signs" that urban churches tend to have in common that are emblematic of the improving health of these congregations.[75] One of the vital signs that Harper identifies is the ability of leaders to capitalize on human gifts and what sociologists call "social capital". He asserts that this is the inner resource that lifts up new and indigenous leadership; it is the human asset that helps empower previously uninvolved people.[76]

Harvey Conn and Manuel Ortiz, in *Urban Ministry: The Kingdom, the City and the People of God,* similarly identified several contextual traits of urban leaders and proposed three types of urban leaders — relocated leaders, indigenous leaders, and multi-ethnic leaders.[77] According to Conn and Ortiz, relocated leaders enter the urban community from a different environment or culture, such as a suburban or rural context. Indigenous leaders are those who have grown up in the city and belong to a certain culture. And multi-ethnic leaders are

---

[74] Jason Byassee, "Strategies for Urban Ministry" in *The Christian Century* (Chicago, IL: The Christian Century) March 8, 2008), 22-29.

[75] Nile Harper, *Urban Churches: Vital Signs - Beyond Charity, Toward Justice* (Grand Rapids: Eerdmans Publishing, 1999), 1.

[76] Harper, *Urban Churches*, 10.

[77] Harvie M. Conn and Manuel Ortiz, *Urban Ministry: The Kingdom of God, the City and the People of God* (Downers Grove, IL: InterVarsity Press, 2001), 378-397.

typically ministering in a racially-ethnically diverse context and might work with other leaders in a local church.

Conn and Ortiz also asserted that the critical impact that context has on leadership requires that the three kinds of church leaders be distinguished. Apart from understanding the important role of context in urban ministry, it is not possible to distinguish these different kinds of leaders. Would-be leaders and their churches need to be aware of these differences so that they can consider them in their preparation for ministry.[78]

Given the unique qualities and dynamics of urban communities today, urban ministries and the leaders who serve in these contexts must be uniquely equipped with relational and technical skills to lead in facilitating community wholeness and flourishing. Urban ministry seeks to address the particular felt needs that exist among people in defined urban contexts. This is often seen in addressing people's tangible felt needs for education, employment, health care, housing, safety/policing, technology, and transportation.

But urban ministry also entails addressing the common human spiritual strivings of seeing and experiencing God in communities through the work of urban ministry in fulfilling God's mission through acts of worship, discipleship, fellowship, mission, and evangelism. Urban ministry entails promoting and being agents of God's love, peace, blessing, and hope among people in urban contexts.

---

[78] Conn and Ortiz, *Urban Ministry*, 379-380.

# CHAPTER FOUR
## NEHEMIAH: A BIBLICAL MODEL FOR TRANSFORMATIONAL LEADERSHIP

*So we rebuilt the wall until all of it reached half its height, for the people worked with all their hearts. (Nehemiah 4:6)*

Several biblical figures and their leadership shed light on the dynamics of transformational Christian leadership in the 21st-century. Two of these figures are Nehemiah who led in rebuilding the walls of Jerusalem, and Paul who was a transformational leader in missional ministry and church planting during the early church era. In this chapter, Nehemiah's leadership will be analyzed through a study of the Book of Nehemiah, and in the next chapter, Paul's leadership will be analyzed through a study of the Pauline Epistles, to glean insights into transformational leadership and ministry in urban contexts in the 21st-century.

### Nehemiah and Rebuilding the Walls of Jerusalem

The case of Nehemiah is a study of how leadership, teamwork, and collaboration can result in accomplishing challenging organizational tasks and provides insight into transformational leadership and ministry in urban contexts in the 21st-century.

The book of Nehemiah forms a unity with the preceding book of Ezra. Most scholars believe that it is likely that Ezra-Nehemiah was compiled as one book by Ezra, Nehemiah, or someone else using the memoirs of Ezra and Nehemiah along with other sources.[79] As a sequel to the book of Ezra, the book of Nehemiah reports the third return to Jerusalem in 445 BCE.

According to Mervin Breneman, Ezra stresses the religious restoration of the remnant when writing about the erection of the altar, the building of the temple, and reading and keeping the Law (the Torah).[80] Breneman points out that the book of Ezra indicates that the Law was not read so much to bring a reform; that was already begun earlier by Ezra's prayer and confession. Rather the Law was read as part of the liturgical celebration by the revived community.[81]

After Nehemiah heard of the plight of his people in Jerusalem and that the city was in ruins without a wall of defense against their enemies, he asked the Persian king's permission to go to Jerusalem to see what could be done. This was granted and Nehemiah was sent out as a governor of Judah with all the privileges of the post of governor of a province in the satrapy of Trans-Euphrates.[82] Herbert Marbury points out that the king dispatched Nehemiah with imprimatur to function as governor of the province. Meanwhile, the narrator informs the reader that Nehemiah holds deep loyalties to the Jerusalem collective. Nehemiah's concern for the sorry condition of the infrastructure of Jerusalem prompts him to leave the Persian

---

[79] Mervin Breneman, *The New American Commentary: An Exegetical and Theological Exposition of Holy Scripture – Ezra, Nehemiah, Esther,* (Nashville, TN: Broadman and Holman Publisher, 1993), 37.

[80] Breneman, *The New American Commentary: An Exegetical and Theological Exposition of Holy Scripture – Ezra, Nehemiah, Esther,* 43-44.

[81] Breneman, *The New American Commentary: An Exegetical and Theological Exposition of Holy Scripture – Ezra, Nehemiah, Esther,* 44.

[82] Bruce Metzger and Michael Coogan, eds., *The Oxford Companion to the Bible* (Oxford, UK: Oxford University Press, 1993), 553.

court and initiate the rebuilding of the wall (Neh. 1:1-6).[83] That Nehemiah was sent by the Persian king with proper license, protection and provision indicate the favorable timing of Nehemiah's and the people's return to Jerusalem to undertake the rebuilding of the city's walls. (Neh. 2:7-9)

According to his statement, Nehemiah traveled twice from Shushan to Jerusalem. The first journey took place in the 20th year of Artaxerxes I., king of Persia, and lasted until the king's 32nd year (Neh. 2:1; 5:14; 13:6). After this, Nehemiah undertook a second journey to Jerusalem (Neh. 13:6-7). King Artaxerxes reigned from 464 to 424 BCE. So, Nehemiah's first stay lasted from 445 to 433 BCE and the second stay probably followed soon after. The book of Nehemiah can therefore have been composed up to around 400 BCE.[84]

During the period of Israel's exile, Nehemiah was to lead God's people through an extremely difficult construction project in Jerusalem, in which they rebuilt the city's walls. An important observation is that Jerusalem's walls were rebuilt in 52 days, while the oppression of the people and destruction of the city had gone on for 141 years (Neh. 6:15).[85] The reconstruction of the walls remains a remarkable achievement, especially in light of the dispatch with which the project was

---

[83] Herbert Marbury, "Ezra and Nehemiah" in *The Africana Bible: Reading Israel's Scriptures from Africa and the African Diaspora,* Hugh R. Page, Jr. ed. (Minneapolis: Fortress Press, 2010), 280.

[84] Metzger and Coogan, eds., *The Oxford Companion to the Bible,* 553.

[85] Unless otherwise noted, all Scripture citations are from *The Holy Bible,* New International Version, (Colorado Springs, CO: International Bible Society, 1984).

carried out in a mere 52 days.[86] Devising and enacting a plan such as one to rebuild Jerusalem's walls required not only time but leadership and having the right people in place in the right positions (the right team) to accomplish the mission.

Since Nehemiah led in the city of Jerusalem, it can be argued that his ministry was a model for urban ministry in the 21st-century. Mark Gornik proposes that Jerusalem was an urban community that was in serious distress and various principles of leadership and community development were in play to rebuild the walls and rebuild lives.[87] For several years, Gornik served as the founding pastor of New Song Presbyterian Church in the inner city Sandtown-Winchester area in Baltimore, Maryland. Since its founding in 1987, New Song Church has been involved in community revitalization and urban renewal similar to that undertaken by Nehemiah and the people of Jerusalem. Gornik offers a depiction of what was going on in Jerusalem in the days of Nehemiah:

> "Let's get to work" the people proclaim in unison. An urban community is in serious distress – its population is depleted, its economic life depressed, and its buildings reduced to rubble. The trials of daily life are intense, and the struggle to keep hope is difficult. Amidst this reality, a small group of people, recognizing the spiritual and economic dimensions of their plight, organize themselves to rebuild their city and

---

[86] Mark Throntveit, *Ezra-Nehemiah: Interpretation - A Bible Commentary for Teaching and Preaching* (Louisville, KY: Westminster John Knox Press, 1992), 89.

[87] Mark Gornik, "Out of the Ruins" in *To Live in Peace: Biblical Faith and the Changing Inner City* (Grand Rapids, MI: Eerdmans, 2002), 128-162.

communal life. To reach this goal, they pool their skills, marshal resources, both public and private, hold back opposing forces, watch over their labors, pray without ceasing, and resolve internal conflicts. Others said it couldn't be done, but as they overcome the many obstacles that face them, a new urban community rises on the old foundation.[88]

The Nehemiah story points to the importance of transformational leaders having the ability to organize people and resources. While Nehemiah was the leader who first articulated the vision to rebuild, the people confirmed the vision and committed themselves to the task. Many people's gifts, through many circumstances, were necessary to achieve the vision of rebuilding Jerusalem's walls. Accomplishing the vision was not easy. Divisions and hard feelings, combined with outside opposition, oppression, and threats made faithfulness very difficult. Yet, Nehemiah and the people persevered and moved toward the completion of the task.

Observations found in Nehemiah's leadership in rebuilding Jerusalem's walls provide insight into the nature of transformational leadership. These observations include Nehemiah's reliance on and employment of (1) Prayer and research (Neh. 2:12-13); (2) Meetings, strategizing, and team-building (Neh. 2:17-18); (3) Collaborative action and teamwork (Neh. 3:1-32); (4) Facing opposition (Neh. 4:7-12); (5) Reorganizing and re-strategizing (Neh. 4:13-15); and (6) Persistence, resilience, and resourcefulness (Neh. 4: 21-23).

---

[88] Gornik, *To Live in Peace*, 128.

The first observation about Nehemiah's leadership is that there was a *reliance on prayer and research*. After he arrived in Jerusalem, Nehemiah conducted a secret inspection of the city's walls. In other words, he did research on the situation of what had occurred in Jerusalem. It seems that he tried to hide his intentions from the people so the news of his plans would not reach the neighboring enemies. After the inspection, Nehemiah decided to organize the people and rebuild the walls.[89]

John Perkins points out that Nehemiah prayed before he acted. It was not until four months after he heard about the condition of Jerusalem that Nehemiah presented an action plan to the king of Persia. During these four months, Nehemiah prayed and fasted on behalf of the people.[90]

The rebuilding project began with examining Jerusalem's walls. Such careful examination and research were critical for understanding the situation and the task that was before them before any other work began. And such examination and research were also important for understanding what people and other resources would be needed to accomplish the task.

According to Perkins, the foundation of all that was to follow for Nehemiah and the people was laid during the time of prayer. Prayer equips us for action.[91] References to Nehemiah's reliance on prayer can be found throughout the book including in Nehemiah 1:5-11; 2:4-5; 4:4-5; 4:9; 5:19; 6:9; 6:14; 13:14. In Nehemiah 2:12-13, he stated:

---

[89] Metzger and Coogan, *The Oxford Companion to the Bible*, 554.
[90] Perkins, *Restoring At-Risk Communities*, 66.
[91] Perkins, *Restoring At-Risk Communities*, 66.

> I set out during the night with a few others. I had
> not told anyone what my God had put in my heart
> to do for Jerusalem. There were no mounts with
> me except the one I was riding on. By night I went
> out through the Valley Gate toward the Jackal
> Well and the Dung Gate, examining the walls of
> Jerusalem, which had been broken down, and its
> gates, which had been destroyed by fire.

Joseph Daniels asserts that leaders today, as was the case with Nehemiah, must respond to the pockets of their churches and communities that are in ruin, and he writes of the necessity of bathing the church and community, or that which has caused heartbreak, in prayer.[92] He asserts that congregations will be known for either mending the hearts of marginalized persons in the community or as a Christian social club that gathers for an hour or two every Sunday morning. According to Daniels, Nehemiah's ministry and leadership in Jerusalem, an urban context, leads to reflection on ways in which urban churches and leaders can more effectively engage with their communities, and help in leading to rebuilding where necessary.[93]

God has always called leaders. Leaders must hear God's calling to lead and respond to that call. Through prayer, Nehemiah understood his leadership as a calling from God (Neh. 2:12b). He listened and came to see the need. He constantly asked God to provide a vision for him and the people, as he understood that a true vision must come from God. It must be a God-inspired and God-revealed vision. Through prayer,

---

[92] Daniels, *Walking with Nehemiah*, 14.
[93] Daniels, *Walking with Nehemiah*, 14.

Nehemiah also came to know that the vision was "what God has put into my heart" (Neh. 2:12). His (their) vision emerged amid the devastating situation - the destruction of Jerusalem's walls.

The second observation about Nehemiah's leadership is *the importance of meetings, strategizing, and team-building.* Nehemiah was strategic and highly organized. Edwin Yamauchi points out that the "list" contained in Nehemiah 4 names some "forty-one parties" and "forty-two sections" which were focal points of the repairs.[94] Devising and enacting a plan such as one to rebuild Jerusalem's walls required not only time, but leadership, organization, and having the right people and resources in place in the right positions to accomplish the mission. Nehemiah 2:17-18 points to Nehemiah's reliance on meetings, strategizing, and team-building:

> Then I said to them, "You see the trouble we are in: Jerusalem lies in ruins, and its gates have been burned with fire. Come, let us rebuild the walls of Jerusalem, and we will no longer be in disgrace." I also told them about the gracious hand of my God on me and what the king had said to me. They replied, "Let us start rebuilding." So, they began this good work.

John Perkins asserts that in Nehemiah's model of leadership, it is evident that he led the people of Israel to rebuild the walls of Jerusalem with a strategic and methodical process. He suggests that the people of Israel rebuilt the walls of

---

[94] Edwin Yamauchi, "Nehemiah" in *The Expositor's Bible Commentary: Volume 4.* Frank E. Gaebelein, ed. 678-771 (Grand Rapids, MI: Zondervan, 1988), 692.

Jerusalem because Nehemiah "prayed before he acted, sensed God's timing, counted all potential costs, and did all of his homework."[95] Nehemiah's actions were not impulsive but were a consequence of critical contemplation. His leadership informs an approach to community engagement/organizing in urban ministry contexts for the transformation of people and communities. As ministry leaders pray and assess their communities, they must then develop and implement an action plan for rebuilding.

After hearing from God, Nehemiah listened to the voice of the people, as together they set the course for how they would go about rebuilding the walls. He showed care for their situation and sought the people's input, buy-in, and ownership in establishing plans. He identified with the people, and where they had gifts to help accomplish the rebuilding project. He thought in terms of "we" and "us" (Neh. 2:17-18), and he came to understand and identify with "the trouble we are in" (Neh. 2:17).

Perkins proposes that Nehemiah was also an exemplary community developer, as evidenced by his ability to lead in organizing people and resources to help the walls of Jerusalem be rebuilt.[96] Nehemiah used his discernment for God's timing, counted and calculated the risks/costs, prepared, recognized God's sovereignty, connected with the people, tested his idea, sought God's direction, cooperated with the direction, and refused to get distracted.[97] He knew that he would not be able to accomplish the rebuilding process alone and that it would

---

[95] Perkins, *Restoring At-Risk Communities*, 66.
[96] Perkins, *Restoring At-Risk Communities*, 64.
[97] Perkins, *Restoring At-Risk Communities*, 66-70.

require proper planning and organizing of people and resources before they could begin the work that was before them.

The third observation about Nehemiah's leadership is that *it involved collaborative action.* Raymond Brown pointed out that Nehemiah's leadership demonstrated incarnational priorities like "unity," "individuality," and "unselfishness" in the Israelites taking on their work.[98] Nehemiah 3:1 points to the collaborative approach employed by Nehemiah with other ministry leaders in Jerusalem:

> Eliashib the high priest and his fellow priests went to work and rebuilt the Sheep Gate. They dedicated it and set its doors in place, building as far as the Tower of the Hundred, which they dedicated, and as far as the Tower of Hananel.

This points to the high priest's dedication to the rebuilding project and it shows its religious significance. The walls were regarded as an extension of God's house. This was a cooperative effort. People from all professions and trades helped, coming from many villages and outlying areas of Judah.[99] Within the unity of purpose, there is room for diversity. The variety of builders working side-by-side is striking. Sometimes they are identified by family, other times by profession or place of residence. In general terms, one could say the broad spectrum of the fledgling community was well-

---

[98] Raymond Brown, *The Bible Speaks Today: The Message of Nehemiah* (Downers Grove, IL: Intervarsity Press, 1998), 64-67.
[99] Breneman, *The New American Commentary: An Exegetical and Theological Exposition of Holy Scripture – Ezra, Nehemiah, Esther,* 187.

represented in this list so that all took part in the common task before them.[100]

As Nehemiah gained the people's trust, he was able to develop a team that could collaboratively bring the vision to reality. People shared responsibility for accomplishing the goals leading to fulfilling the vision that had been given. No one person, not even Nehemiah, could have accomplished this vision alone; there needed to be teamwork. He began with a few, then he expanded the team to include virtually everyone. The people committed themselves to the "common good" (Neh. 2:18b).

People's talents were named and used (Neh. 3). Different people worked on different sections of the walls, thus modeling the division of labor. People were assigned to work closest to their homes. But even God's people get tired. They felt the task was taking too much time and was too difficult. There began to be internal disputes. But Nehemiah was able to find ways to alleviate their concerns and helped them stay focused on the vision.

The fourth observation of Nehemiah's leadership was that *there was a willingness and ability to face opposition.* Nehemiah 4:7-9 provides a characterization of the opposition that Nehemiah and the people faced:

> But when Sanballat, Tobiah, the Arabs, the Ammonites, and the people of Ashdod heard that the repairs to Jerusalem's walls had gone ahead and that the gaps were being closed, they were

---

[100] Throntveit, *Ezra-Nehemiah: Interpretation - A Bible Commentary for Teaching and Preaching,* 77-78.

very angry. They all plotted together to come and fight against Jerusalem and stir up trouble against it. But we prayed to our God and posted a guard day and night to meet this threat.

Mark Throntveit points out that the account of the opposition that Nehemiah and the people faced (Neh. 4:7-9) is preceded in verse 6 with a testament to the perseverance of the Jews: "So we rebuilt the wall, and all the wall was joined together to half its height; for the people had a mind to work."[101] According to Throntveit, Nehemiah 4:7-9 ff. outlines a basic pattern of the methods used by the Israelites to resist opposition: (1) The enemies band together intending "to fight against Israel" (4:7-8). (2) The people call upon God for help before arming themselves (4:9). (3) The Lord frustrates the intentions of the enemies, whose courage fails them (4:15). (4) Trumpets are employed in battle summons (4:18-19).[102]

As they rebuilt the walls, they were ridiculed, mocked, and plotted against. Their enemies did everything possible to discourage them, and threatened to tell untrue stories about Nehemiah. Against such resistance, he and the people persisted. He knew he was "doing great work" (Neh. 6:3), and could not come down from the wall to debate with their adversaries. He and the people persisted even when adversity came. Effective leaders and their teams are resilient and persistent and persevere when adversity comes.

[101] Throntveit, *Ezra-Nehemiah: Interpretation - A Bible Commentary for Teaching and Preaching*, 79.
[102] Throntveit, *Ezra-Nehemiah: Interpretation - A Bible Commentary for Teaching and Preaching*, 79.

Insults and criticism can sting and can be distracting and discouraging while trying to accomplish a mission and realize a vision. Nehemiah had critics as he led a team to rebuild Jerusalem's walls. Amid criticism, he prayed *"Hear us, our God, for we are despised. Turn their insults back on their heads"* (Neh. 4:4). What leaders can do amidst criticism is take time to step back, evaluate the good and bad in the criticism that might come, stay in prayer, trust God, and then persistently continue to organize the work that has been put before them.

The fifth observation that can be made from Nehemiah's leadership in rebuilding Jerusalem's walls is that there was the ability *to reorganize and re-strategize.* In Nehemiah 4:13-15, he states:

> Therefore, I stationed some of the people behind the lowest points of the wall at the exposed places, posting them by families, with their swords, spears, and bows. After I looked things over, I stood up and said to the nobles, the officials, and the rest of the people, "Don't be afraid of them. Remember the Lord, who is great and awesome, and fight for your families, your sons and your daughters, your wives and your homes." When our enemies heard that we were aware of their plot and that God had frustrated it, we all returned to the wall, each to our work.

Nehemiah led in taking definitive action. He had to sacrifice some labor from building the wall, but the precaution was necessary. Grouping people by family strengthened the motivation to fight (Neh. 4:14).[103] In the face of danger, Nehemiah set up certain measures of defense for the workers. He set armed groups in open places under the cover of the wall where they could maneuver more freely if attacked. Armed men also took their places among the workers.[104]

It is easy for people to forget the purpose behind the vision even as they work to fulfill it. Nehemiah and the people's vision was to rebuild the walls, but the walls were not the most important part of the vision. The rebuilding of the walls was a means to a larger purpose. What Nehemiah and the people's work was really about was reclaiming their identity as people of faith. What was at stake was not just rebuilding physical walls, but also, rebuilding the people's lives and relationships with God (Neh. 8; 12:27). Nehemiah had to ensure that the people were reminded of their faithful past. Because their rebuilding task was tied to a greater purpose, they put their hearts into their work and were able to complete the task in 52 days (Neh. 6:15-16).

The sixth and final observation about Nehemiah's leadership is that *it involved persistence, resilience, and resourcefulness.* John Perkins states that "Nehemiah was a businessman and administrator, not a prophet or a priest. He was a community developer; with his leadership, his people rebuilt the walls of Jerusalem."[105]

---

[103] Breneman, *The New American Commentary: An Exegetical and Theological Exposition of Holy Scripture – Ezra, Nehemiah, Esther,* 197-198.

[104] Charles Fritsch, "The Book of Nehemiah", in *The Interpreter's One-Volume Commentary of the Bible,* Charles Layman, ed. (Nashville: Abingdon Press, 1971), 229.

[105] Perkins, *Restoring At-Risk Communities,* 66-70.

Perkins highlights prayer, wisdom, deep listening, and critical observation as critical aspects of how Nehemiah assessed the community's needs. Perkins then names planning, community organizing, mobilizing, and executing to accomplish common goals. Here is a reminder of the necessity of having a clear sense of motivation and determination. Nehemiah spoke of the persistence, resilience, and resourcefulness that he and the people of Israel possessed in Nehemiah 4:21-23:

> So, we continued the work with half the men holding spears, from the first light of dawn till the stars came out. At that time, I also said to the people, "Have every man and his helper stay inside Jerusalem at night, so they can serve us as guards by night and as workers by day." Neither I, nor my brothers, nor my men, nor the guards with me took off our clothes; each had his weapon, even when he went for water.

The men and their helpers were asked to serve as guards at night and work during the day. Any vision that God gives takes persistence, resilience, and perseverance to be fulfilled. It has been intimated that a vision that is of God is too big to be accomplished by humans alone. This means that God's vision requires the persistent presence of God, the persistent presence of teamwork, and the resilience and resourcefulness to make adjustments along the way.

With Nehemiah and the people of Israel working through the dynamics of conflict, opposition, and discord, their unity of purpose and collaboration needed to be consistent, and this seems to be key in any leadership context in the movement toward transformation.

In summary, Nehemiah demonstrated several transformational qualities important for effective leadership in his urban context that could apply to transformational leadership in urban contexts today. Some of the transformational leadership qualities identified in Nehemiah include the following: (1) Transformational leaders have a genuine concern for the well-being of their people. Nehemiah said, "And I asked them concerning the Jews who escaped, who had survived the exile, and concerning Jerusalem" (Neh. 1:2). (2) Transformational leaders show care toward their people. Nehemiah intimates in Nehemiah 3:4, "As soon as I heard these words I sat down and wept and mourned for days, and I continued fasting and praying before the God of heaven." When he got the distressing news about the condition of Jerusalem, Nehemiah found himself mourning, weeping, and praying for his people. (3) Transformational leaders know and are dependent on God. In Nehemiah 1:5, he said, "O Lord God of heaven, the great and awesome God who keeps covenant and steadfast love with those who love him and keep his commandments." Even though Israel was being judged by God, Nehemiah still focused on the promise of God's love for them. (4) Transformational leaders identify with those they lead. He prayed in Nehemiah 1:6 "let your ear be attentive and your eyes open, to hear the prayer of your servant that I now pray before you day and night for the people of Israel your servants, confessing the sins of the people of Israel, which we have sinned against you. Even I and my father's house have sinned." In his prayer, there isn't an us/them dichotomy, it is "we" who need God's leading. (5) Transformational leaders lead with humility. Nehemiah's prayer throughout Nehemiah 1 reflects a level of humility to which all leaders should aspire. He didn't think of himself as being better than the people of Israel but identified with them.

Like Nehemiah and the people of his day, we are responsible for rebuilding the broken walls of our communities. Leaders and churches in urban contexts today are called to bring healing, wholeness, and hope to their communities through the power of Jesus Christ. This is an intentional work that requires sincerity, sacrifice, conviction, courage, and commitment.

# CHAPTER FIVE
## PAUL: A BIBLICAL MODEL FOR THE TRANSFORMATIONAL LEADERSHIP

*"Do not conform to the pattern of this world, but be transformed by the renewing of your mind. Then you will be able to test and approve what God's will is—his good, pleasing, and perfect will."*
*(Romans 12:2)*

Similar to Nehemiah, Paul's life, ministry, and leadership provide a clear indication of the qualities necessary for effective transformational leadership. Indeed, Paul's ability to understand different cultures and contexts helped him to be adaptive as he needed to target his life and teaching to the needs of those he led (1 Cor. 9:20). This is to say that Paul changed his leadership style to meet different needs. For example, he wanted to deal with the Galatians, face-to-face, so they could know the full force of his apostolic concern (Gal. 4:20), but he spared the Corinthians a painful visit, preferring to write (2 Cor. 1:23–2:4). This shows that Paul understood people and their needs, and at points, he adapted his leadership to fit different situations.

According to C. Michelle Venable-Ridley, Paul, a first-century non-Palestinian Jew, was born in the city of Tarsus, a naval installation in the Roman Empire around 5-15 CE. Born to a family of impressive Jewish heritage, Paul was named after the tribe's most illustrious member, King Saul.[106] Paul was "circumcised on the eighth day, of the people of Israel, of the tribe of Benjamin, a Hebrew born of Hebrews; as to the law a Pharisee" (Philippians 3:5).

The exact date of Paul's birth is uncertain. However, he is referred to as a young man (*neanios*) at the stoning of Stephen (the death of Stephen cannot have been much before 31 CE; Acts 7:58), and Paul calls himself an old man (*presbytes*) in Philemon 9, around 52-54 CE. Correlating these points of reference with his meeting with Gallio (50-52 CE) in Corinth and his martyrdom under Nero (54-68 CE), we can estimate his birth around 5-15 CE.[107]

In many ways, Paul's life and experiences transcended culture. He was a Jewish Pharisee, who would be touched by Jesus and become a Christian convert. He was a Roman Citizen, a Judeo-Christian, a born-again Christian, a lawyer, a theologian, a philosopher, a missionary, a church planter, and a pastor. Paul preached to Jews and Gentiles, the richer and the poorer.

N.T. Wright asserts that a great deal can be learned from who Paul was, and his experiences as an apostle, theologian, church planter and leader in the early church help in understanding church leadership today.[108] For Paul, there was no question about the starting point. It was always Jesus: Jesus the shocking fulfillment of Israel's hopes; Jesus as the

---

[106] C. Michelle Venable-Ridley, "Paul and the African American Community" in *Embracing the Spirit: Womanist Perspectives on Hope, Salvation, and Transformation,* Emilie M. Townes, ed. (Maryknoll, NY: Orbis, 1997), 214.
[107] Venable-Ridley, "Paul and the African American Community", 214.
[108] N.T. Wright, *Paul: A Biography* (New York: Harper, 2018), 399-432.

genuinely human being, the true "image"; Jesus the embodiment of Israel's God – so that, without leaving Jewish monotheism, one would worship and invoke Jesus as Lord *within*, not alongside, the service of the living and true God.[109]

Paul was an example of a leader transformed by Christ who went forth to engage in transformational leadership. According to Ursula King, Paul's transformation began with his conversion experience with Christ on the road to Damascus. According to King, Paul's experience on the Damascus Road changed him from an enemy of Christianity into an ardent supporter of the early Christians, and he became one of the strongest witnesses to the power of the spirit of Christ, *"in whom we live, move and have our being"* (Acts 17:28).[110]

Michael Gorman points out that both Acts and Paul's letters describe Paul's unexpected and unmerited encounter with the resurrected Jesus, sometime in the mid-thirties of the first century (1 Cor. 15:9-10). Although Acts gives more details, Paul supplies the essentials, saying that the resurrected Jesus appeared to him as he had previously done to others, apparently one of the chief criteria of apostleship (1 Cor. 9:1; 15:8). This was divine revelation, and *apokalypsis* (Galatians 1:15-16), the defining moment of Paul's life.[111]

Paul's conversion experience is described three times in the Book of Acts (chapters 9, 22, and 26). Scholars assume that Luke wrote Acts around 85 CE, about twenty years after Paul's ministry. Paul's account, in his letter to the Galatians, was:

---

[109] Wright, *Paul: A Biography*, 400.

[110] Ursula King, *Christian Mystics: Their Lives and Legacies Throughout the Ages* (Mahwah, NJ: Hidden Spring, 2001), 13.

[111] Michael J. Gorman, *Reading Paul* (Eugene, OR: Cascade Books, 2008), 14.

*"The Gospel which I preach... came through the revelation of Jesus Christ"* (Acts 1:11-12).

Paul described himself as "a man in Christ", affirming a deep union with the Divine which does not negate his own identity but enables him to live within the divine nature itself: *"I live, now not I; but Christ lives within me"* (Gal. 2:20). He also sings the praises of active love, of charity, inspired by the fire of divine love, and outlines a vision of the cosmic Christ, the Christ who *"is all and is in all"* (Colossians 3:11).[112]

Not only was Paul's way of thinking transformed by his mystical experience, but so too, was his way of being in the world. Suddenly the persecutor — and possibly murderer — of Christians is Christ's "chosen vessel," sent *"to carry my name before the Gentiles and kings and the sons of Israel"* (Acts 9:15).[113]

Brad Braxton asserts that Paul's encounter with Christ compelled Paul to reevaluate every aspect of his identity. Before this encounter, Paul's Pharisaic heritage had been his stance and pride.[114] His experience with Christ compelled him to rethink certain aspects of his Pharisaic heritage. However, he never relinquished his Jewish heritage. Daniel Boyarin insists that Paul lived and died convinced that he was a Jew living out Judaism.[115]

---

[112] King, *Christian Mystics: Their Lives and Legacies Throughout the Ages*, 13.

[113] King, *Christian Mystics: Their Lives and Legacies Throughout the Ages*, 13.

[114] Brad Braxton, *Preaching Paul* (Nashville, TN: Abingdon Press, 2004), 47.

[115] Daniel Boyarin, *A Radical Jew: Paul and the Politics of Identity* (Berkley: University of California Press, 1994), 2.

According to Marcus Borg and John Dominic Crossan, after his conversion, Paul's identity became an identity "in Christ." He saw Judaism anew in the light of Jesus.[116] Borg and Crossan assert that Paul's transformation involved an "identity transplant" — his old identity was replaced by a new identity "in Christ.". We have in mind an analogy to modern medicine's heart transplant, in which an old heart is replaced by a new heart. In Paul's case, his spirit —the old Paul—had been replaced by the Spirit of Christ.[117]

Paul's teaching on the gifts of the Spirit, from 1 Corinthians 12–14 is an extension of his identity transplant "in Christ." Here Borg and Crossan reflect on the implications of Paul's thoughts on love, *"And now faith, hope, and love abide, these three; and the greatest of these is love"* (1 Cor. 13:13). The love of which Paul speaks is a spiritual gift, not simply an act of will, not something we decide to do, not simply good advice for couples and others. Rather, as a spiritual gift, love is the most important result (and evidence) of a Spirit transplant. As the primary fruit of the Spirit, it is also the criterion by which the other gifts are evaluated.[118]

Harvey Egan asserts that Paul gave himself fully to the love of God in Christ and believed others could do likewise.[119] From the very depths of his being, Paul experienced and surrendered to the love of God in Christ. For him, the Lord was

---

[116] Marcus J. Borg and John Dominic Crossan, *The First Paul: Reclaiming the Radical Visionary behind the Church's Conservative Icon* (New York: HarperCollins, 2009), 26.

[117] Borg and Crossan, *The First Paul*, 26.

[118] Borg and Crossan, *The First Paul*, 138.

[119] Harvey D. Egan, *Christian Mysticism: The Future of a Tradition* (New York: Pueblo Publishing, 1984), 26–27.

the Spirit (2 Cor. 3:17). Pauline mysticism is emphatically Christ-directed; "to live," for Paul, "is Christ" (Phil. 1:21). For Paul, it was almost self-evident that because of Christ and his Spirit, all Christians had access to an experience of God in their lives. Although Paul spoke of the "mature" in faith (1 Cor. 2:6) and the "spiritual" (1 Cor. 2:15), he expected mature faith among all Christians. The Holy Spirit granted all Christians a "surpassing knowledge" (Eph. 3:19), the "fullness of knowledge" (Eph. 1:17), and in this way proved to us that we are "[children] of God" (Rom. 8:14) who can also call God, "Abba, Father" (Rom. 8:15). Christ's Spirit would pray in us "with sighs too deep for words" (Rom. 8:26).[120]

Linked intimately to a loving knowledge of the crucified and risen Christ is a "secret and hidden wisdom of God" (1 Cor. 2:7), a peace beyond all understanding (Phil. 4:7), and a supreme consolation (2 Cor. 1:5). Those living in Christ's Spirit experience a richer way of life (Eph. 1:8–9) filled with love, joy, peace, self-control, gentleness, patience, and kindness (Gal. 5:22) that enables them to bear each other's burdens (Gal. 6:2). As Paul said: *"What no eye has seen, nor ear heard, nor the [human] heart conceived, what God has prepared for those who love him, God has revealed to us through the Spirit"* (1 Cor. 2:9–10). Time and again, Paul spoke of being "in Christ." For him, moreover, *"it is no longer I who live, but Christ lives in me"* (Gal. 2:20).[121]

A key theological construct that is at work as it regards transformational leadership and Paul's life and ministry is the

---

[120] Egan, *Christian Mysticism,* 26–27.
[121] Egan, *Christian Mysticism,* 26–27.

term, transformation. Transformation can be seen through changed thinking, behaviors, and habits among leaders and those being led. It implies a move from what is (actual) to a preferred state (aspirational) — that is, God's preferred future for our lives. Paul's encouragement in Romans 12:1-2 comes to mind:

> Therefore, I urge you, brothers and sisters, given God's mercy, to offer your bodies as a living sacrifice, holy and pleasing to God—this is your true and proper worship. Do not conform to the pattern of this world, but be transformed by the renewing of your mind. Then you will be able to test and approve what God's will is — God's good, pleasing, and perfect will.

Craig Hill asserts that in Romans 12:2b, there is evidence that the new, eschatological righteousness overmasters humanity's ancient, fallen nature: believers experience a 'renewal of their minds' so that they may discern what is the will of God — what is good and acceptable and perfect.[122] For Paul, it is no less than a return, a 'conforming' to the original order, the re-creation of human minds not subjected to futility (Rom. 8:20). Paul does not expect his readers to obtain such an exalted capability on their own. Rather, he believes that as possessors of the Spirit, they are already

[122] Craig C. Hill, "Romans" in *The Oxford Bible Commentary*, John Bartman, and John Muddiman, eds. (Oxford, UK: Oxford University Press, 2001), 1104.

equipped to live lives *'holy and acceptable to God'* (Rom. 12:1).[123]

Ursula King asserts that while the Gospels describe Christ's life, death, and resurrection, the Pauline Epistles bear witness to an intense and profoundly transforming faith, rooted both in powerful personal experience and in the community of the early disciples, which later became the Christian Church.[124]

To conform to the world means essentially to move away from the ways of God. It means to stay mired in the fallenness and brokenness in our societal midst. But to be transformed means to experience the re-molding of the broken realities that are in and around us.

Paul said, "don't be conformed to (don't try to be like) the world, but be transformed (be changed) by the renewing (the changing) of your minds." Eugene Peterson's rendering of this verse from *The Message* translation of the Bible is helpful: *"Don't be so well-adjusted to your culture that you fit into it without thinking. Instead, fix your attention on God. You'll be changed from the inside out."*[125]

Thomas Hoyt asserts that Paul called for the transformation of the mind because he knew that actions are generated by attitudes. This transformation is not a one-time event but a constant struggle. The Christian agenda is not to be determined by current secular standards. The Christian's

---

[123] Hill, "Romans", 1104.

[124] King, *Christian Mystics: Their Lives and Legacies Throughout the Ages*, 13.

[125] Eugene Peterson, *The Message: The Bible in Contemporary Language* (Colorado Springs, CO: NavPress, 2003), 2052.

standards are determined by the coming new age as sustained by the Holy Spirit.[126]

According to Lisa Bowens, Paul, in Romans 12:1-2, reminds his audience that the ethical principles of Christianity are important to follow, and one cannot just be a Christian in name, but a Christian lifestyle must follow that name. Just as Paul presented these ethical principles in his day, even though they were not popular, so, too, must believers today.[127]

About sixty years ago, Martin Luther King, Jr. preached a sermon entitled, "Transformed Nonconformist." King based his message on the text from Paul's letter to the Church in Rome, where in Romans 12:2, Paul reminded the Christians in Rome that they were to "be not conformed to the world but be transformed by the renewing of (their) minds."[128]

The context for King's message, this matter of transformed nonconformity, was the American Civil Rights movement of the mid-20th -century, and the need for leadership in the church and society that would stay the course in seeking to transform society and deliver America from the racial division, economic disparity, and other social maladies that plagued the nation then.

Concerning this matter of conformity and the call to transformation, King wrote that "Success, recognition, and conformity are the bywords of the modern world where

---

[126] Thomas L. Hoyt, Jr., "Romans" in *True to Our Native Lane: An African American New Testament Commentary*, Brian K. Blount, ed. (Minneapolis, MN: Fortress Press, 2007), 268.

[127] Lisa M. Bowens, *African American Readings of Paul: Reception, Resistance and Transformation* (Grand Rapids, MI: William B. Eerdmans, 2020), 242.

[128] Martin Luther King, Jr., "Transformed Nonconformist", in *Strength to Love* (Minneapolis, MN: Fortress, 2010), 11-20.

everyone seems to crave the anesthetizing security of being identified with the majority… Despite the prevailing tendency to conform, we as Christians have the mandate to be nonconformists."[129]

King's message comes to mind when giving thought to what it means to be a transformed and transformational leader in the church today. His notion of transformed non-conformity leads to reflection on what it means to be a transformational and adaptive leader today, and what transformed, adaptive leadership needs to look like into the future.

Transformed non-conformity is a primary challenge for the 21st-century church and its leaders, particularly in the post-COVID-19 period. In today's nano-second, drive-through, instant message, instant everything world, it is the leader's challenge to lead in changing the realities in our churches and communities in ways that make sense for today. Today's leaders must lead in ways where they are not subsumed by every fad, quick-fix, church guru, consultant, program, seminar, workshop, conference, webinar, podcast, and new idea that comes along.

As a transformed, transformational leader, Paul demonstrated the importance of flexibility, fluidity, and resiliency in his leadership. In seeking to share the Gospel message in various contexts, he sought to be a "Greek to the Greeks, and a Jew to the Jewish" persons with whom he ministered. In (2 Cor. 12:7-9), he talked of being given a "thorn in his flesh:

> Therefore, to keep me from becoming conceited, I was given a thorn in my flesh, a messenger of

---

[129] King, *Strength Love,* 12.

Satan, to torment me. Three times I pleaded with the Lord to take it away from me. But he said to me, "My grace is sufficient for you, for my power is made perfect in weakness."

There is no clear evidence of what or who the "thorn" was, but it can be surmised that the imagery of a thorn in Paul's flesh pertained to real and persistent pain and pernicious difficulties that he faced. At other points, Paul talked about being *"hard-pressed on every side but not in despair... being persecuted but not in distress"* (2 Cor. 4:8-9). He was acquainted with living through difficult, painful times. Amid these stated realities, Paul summed them up by saying that *"we are more than conquerors through Christ who loves us"* (Rom. 8:37).

Here is a reminder of the need for transformational qualities among today's leaders – qualities of flexibility, fluidity, and resiliency that will result in the persons with whom leaders serve being empowered toward greater avenues of Christian discipleship and witness.

Paul's letters also depict countless personal connections and relationships. Romans 16 alone mentions thirty-five people by name, and several others through their associations with those named.[130] His leadership was relational, personal, and directed toward the good of others. It was located and exercised within a network of relationships, which he valued and fostered. Some of these relationships were asymmetrical—where he had a role and authority that set him apart. Significantly, all relationships also had symmetrical elements, where Paul was

---

[130] Hill, "Romans" in *The Oxford Bible Commentary*, 1105.

one among many—fathers, apostles, workers, servants—and where he shared a mutual identity and bonds with fellow believers. More broadly, Paul's letters were not 'form letters' but targeted letters, written to specific people in specific churches in specific locations and differing cultural and ministerial settings. His commitment to personal relationships and contextualized ministry, and coming alongside people, lies behind his appeals and exhortations for certain beliefs and conduct to transform lives and the church.

As a leader, Paul sought to lead by example. E. P. Sanders in *Paul: A Very Short Introduction*, asserts that just as Paul saw himself as exemplifying the correct behavior, so he also saw himself as a model of exertion.[131] He wrote to the church at Thessalonica, *"You remember, brothers, our toils and drudgery. Working night and day in order not to burden any of you, we proclaimed to you the Gospel of God"* (1 Thes. 2:9).

According to Michael Gorman, Paul's goal as an evangelist and pastor was to call others to the same Jesus and thus the same experience of God (as was his). He did and still does, through his preaching, example, and letter-writing.[132] Effort characterized not only Paul's manual labor to support himself (1 Cor. 4:12), but also his activity as an apostle: he worked harder than any of the other apostles (1 Cor. 15:10), and he dreaded the thought that he might have labored in vain. (1 Thes. 3). He had special respect for other leaders of the new movement who worked hard (1 Thes. 5:12). Paul fully espoused

---

[131] E. P. Sanders, *Paul: Very Short Introduction* (Oxford, UK: Oxford University Press, 1991), 119.
[132] Gorman, *Reading Paul*, 20.

and observed a 'work ethic' as long as the goal was the right one.[133]

In summary, from Paul, we learn that transformational church leaders today must be prayerful and discerning, discreet and strategic in determining what will be needed to lead churches and communities toward the specific vision — the preferred future — that God intends. They must resist the temptation to copy and imitate every successful mega-church or corporate leader who comes along. They must be pastoral and theological, love everybody while listening to them and leading them, and stay true to the Gospel while relating (not conforming) to an ever-changing world. Theirs must be a life of changing, growing, improvising, and adapting as they seek to be God's transformed agents of helping to transform lives, communities, and the world.

---

[133] Sanders, *Paul: Very Short Introduction,* 119.

# CHAPTER SIX
## TRANSFORMED TO LEAD, PART I : BIBLICAL AND THEOLOGICAL PERSPECTIVES ON TRANSFORMATIONAL LEADERSHIP

*As the time approached for him to be taken up to heaven, Jesus resolutely set out for Jerusalem. (Luke 9:21)*

In "Decentralization and the Shared Leadership of the New Testament," Justin Irving asserts that "the worldview of New Testament Christians led to a theologically informed practice of leadership that was distinctively decentralized or shared."[134] According to Irving, even in cases of individual leaders like Timothy and Titus, their roles in Ephesus and Crete accordingly were in collaboration with Paul and sending churches, and were meant as transitional roles in which plural forms of leadership would be established. Note Paul's words to Titus confirming this: *"For this reason, I let you in Crete, that you would set in order what remains and appoint elders (a plural, collaborative form of leadership) in every city as I directed you"* (Titus 1:5).[135]

Also, theologically, transformational leadership is informed by an affirmation of a Trinitarian God. Irving asserts

---

[134] Justin Irving, "Decentralization and the Shared Leadership of the New Testament," ML-924P-30 Spring, 2021, Teams, Groups and the Transforming Leader (April 8, 2004) (paper presented, Bethel Theological Seminary, St. Paul, MN, Spring 2021), 1.

[135] Irving, "Decentralization and the Shared Leadership of the New Testament", 7.

that the Bible is robustly Trinitarian.[136] To support this claim, he points out that George Cladis notes that the understanding of God as Trinity serves as a master image affecting how relationships and community are thought about.[137] According to Cladis, "all Christians are brought into fellowship with the triune God", thus creating the context for relationships and collaboration within the church.

The perichoretic nature and notion of the Trinity (perichoresis) speak to the consistency of the three persons of the Trinity found throughout the Creeds and other Christian teachings. This also speaks to the relationship of the three persons of the Trinity — God the Father (creator), Son (savior/redeemer), and Holy Spirit (sustainer).

If, on the other hand, we affirm that the very nature of God is to seek out the deepest possible communion and friendship with every last creature, and if through the doctrine of the Trinity we do our best to articulate the mystery of God for us, then preaching and pastoral practice will fit naturally with the particulars of the Christian life. Ecclesial life, sacramental life, and ethical life... will be seen clearly as forms of Trinitarian life: living God's life with one another.[138]

Several observations of transformational leadership in the early church as found in Acts 1-11; 17:1-9; and 1 Thessalonians, gleaned from the life of Paul and others provide

---

[136] Irving, "Decentralization and the Shared Leadership of the New Testament", 19.

[137] George Cladis, *Leading the Team-Based Church* (San Francisco: Jossey-Bass, 1999), 92-94.

[138] Catherine Lacugna, *God for Us: The Trinity and Christian Life* (San Francisco: HarperCollins, 1973), 411.

insight into the nature of transformational leadership and have implications for leading in 21st-century ministry settings.

The first, perhaps most obvious observation is that amidst uncertainty in the society of that day, before his ascension, Jesus pointed to the power that would come through the Holy Spirit, when he said in Acts 1:8, *"But you will receive power when the Holy Spirit will come upon you, and you will be my witnesses in Jerusalem, in all Judea and Samaria and to the ends of the earth."*

Second, there is the sense that leaders in the early church quickly understood the importance of community, collaboration, and organizing people for the work of mission and ministry. Acts 2:44 states that *"all who believed were together, and they held all things in common."*

Third, transformational leadership can be seen in those who were chosen to serve and the specific assignments they were given. Acts 6 points to the seven who were chosen, and how they stood before the apostles who prayed for them and laid hands on them.

Fourth, Paul, Silas, and Timothy's experiences in Acts 17:1-11 and 1 Thessalonians 1 are cases in point of the effects of transformational leadership on communities and institutions. As Acts 17:4 indicates, *"some of them (who heard and encountered Paul and Silas) were persuaded and joined Paul and Silas."* The transition among much of the status quo from a Jewish religious worldview, to a Christian religious worldview and life in Christ, is one through which Paul, Silas, and Timothy found themselves leading. In 1 Thessalonians 1:3, Paul, Silas, and Timothy intimate to those serving and leading in Thessalonica, *"we remember… your work produced by faith, your labor prompted by love, and your endurance inspired by hope..."*

Jesus' call of his disciples also serves as a biblical basis and example of transformational leadership development. His model of leadership as he ministered in urban contexts - from Nazareth to Samaria and into Jerusalem — contained essentially three components. First, Jesus gathered persons by identifying those who possessed particular gifts. Secondly, Jesus built relationships, nurtured, mentored, coached, and discipled the persons whom he had identified and gathered. Thirdly, Jesus sought to further develop the gifts of these persons so that they would become empowered leaders, thus replicating and scaling the process of leadership development, and what would become the model for apostolic succession as seen most clearly in Peter, James, and John's preaching and leadership after Jesus' death, and with the formation of the early church, and leadership development therein.

Matthew 9:36-38 points to Jesus as a servant-leader who called and equipped others, *"Seeing the people, he felt compassion for them, because they were distressed and dispirited like sheep without a shepherd."* Then he said to his disciples, *"The harvest is plentiful, but the laborers are few. Therefore, beseech the Lord of the harvest to send out workers to his harvest."*

The image of God's people as a flock without a shepherd is a familiar one in the Old Testament (Numbers 27:17; 1 Kings 22:17; Ezekiel 34) and is a reminder that Jesus was not concerned merely with the individual, but recognized that persons of faith can live and flourish only within the context of people of God whose Shepherd, God had appointed him to be. But the work of shepherding God's flock requires co-workers, or to change the figure, as Matthew does, the harvest, which will bring to the close, an age, and establish the kingdom of God and requires laborers. It is to share in the work of God that the disciples are called.[139]

> Matthew 9:36 points out that Jesus was not irritated nor did he attempt to help himself with his leadership, but he was moved with compassion because of the people's condition. Jesus saw persons in the crowds as those who needed help, and he came alongside them and had compassion. Matthew offers the sheep description to help readers more fully understand the heart of Jesus who sought to transform lives. The pastoral/leadership ethic of Jesus was one of a shepherd who would lay down his life in service with/to/for his sheep. As servant-leaders, pastors and leaders must have a similar ethic of caring for and serving with the people that God has placed under their care.

As a transformational servant-leader, Jesus also modeled humility. In *The Selfless Way of Christ*, Henri Nouwen explicated Jesus' experience in the wilderness (Matt. 4:1-11), the temptations that he faced to be relevant, spectacular, and popular, and how Jesus overcame these temptations.[140] According to Nouwen, Jesus practiced "downward mobility" in his life and ministry, which helped him overcome temptations in the wilderness, and throughout his public ministry. The beckoning toward "downward mobility" in the context of a

---

[139] Charles Layman, ed., *The Interpreter's One-Volume Commentary of the Bible* (Nashville, TN: Abingdon Press, 1971), 621-22.

[140] Henri J. M. Nouwen, *The Selfless Way of Christ: Downward Mobility and the Spiritual Life* (New York: Orbis, 2007), 17-44.

culture that values and rewards upward mobility and success serves as a reminder that leaders need to rely on and follow the example of Christ and depend on him to lead ministry and leadership, and that humility, prayer, and community/ communal accountability are key firewalls against self-centered, self-serving forms of leadership.

According to Carlyle Fielding Stewart, a prerequisite of empowerment and numerical growth within the church is spiritual growth and empowerment among the clergy and laity.[141] He points to how Jesus' ministry and leadership demonstrated empowerment in four specific ways.[142] First, Jesus taught people foundational principles of spirituality that enabled them to see their spiritual traditions in new ways and to conceptualize new possibilities of God in new spiritual frameworks.

Secondly, Jesus' ministry transformed people's spiritual perception and understanding of God through personal revelation, intervention, and interaction with people. Encountering Jesus meant that people were compelled to alter their ideas of God.

Thirdly, Jesus transformed the concept of people in relationship with God. They no longer viewed themselves as passive objects of God's will or as people wholly incapable of positively influencing their social environment and milieu. They saw themselves as co-intentional catalysts for positive change.

---

[141] Carlyle Fielding Stewart, III, *The Empowerment Church: Speaking a New Language for Church Growth* (Nashville: Abingdon Press, 2001), 16.
[142] Stewart, *The Empowerment Church*, 23-24.

Fourthly, Jesus directly, as well as vicariously, transformed communities by providing individuals with the spiritual elements of positive change and renewal. Not only did the recipients of Jesus' power and grace experience change within, but their communities were also changed by the power of their testimonies of Christ's work in their lives.

A key point of theological inquiry and reflection as it regards developing transformational leadership is identifying what God's work might entail and look like as transformation occurs in individuals. As was discussed in the previous chapter, the life and ministry of Paul exemplify what virtue could look like in leaders.

Mark McCloskey and Jim Louwsma assert that there is a strong theoretical basis for including virtue as the first step to effective transformational leadership.[143] Transformational leadership is an inherently moral undertaking focused on securing what both leaders and followers agree is good and right.[144]

According to McCloskey and Louwsma, the question becomes, "What standards or virtues are non-negotiable in the character of the transformational leader?" The Greeks, most notably Plato and Aristotle, created much of our vocabulary of virtue. They embraced prudence (practical wisdom and humility), justice (fairness), fortitude (courage), and

---

[143] Mark McCloskey and Jim Louwsma, *The Art of Virtue-based Transformational Leadership: Building Strong Businesses, Organizations, and Families* (Bloomington, MN: Wordsmith, 2014), 45.
[144] McCloskey and Louwsma, *The Art of Virtue-based Transformational Leadership*, 45.

temperance (moderation) as the moral glue that holds communities together.[145]

Cardinal virtues are a means by which God's transformational work can be accomplished. The principles which underly the cardinal virtues were first explicated by Plato in *Republic*, Book IV, and later expounded upon by theologians like Ambrose, Augustine of Hippo, and Thomas Aquinas as cardinal virtues eventually became theological virtues in Christian contexts.

Ambrose (330–397 CE) is believed to have been the first person to use the term "cardinal virtues". He stated, "And we know that there are four cardinal virtues — temperance, justice, prudence, fortitude."[146] These four virtues were also eventually arrived at in traditional Christian theology: (1) Prudence (or Wisdom) — the capacity to discern appropriate courses of action in particular life situations; (2) Courage — the ability to confront fear, uncertainty, and intimidation. In light of this, Augustine stated that "Hope has two beautiful twin daughters — Anger and Courage. Anger at the way things are, and Courage to change them"; (3) Temperance (Restraint) — the capacity to exercise self-control and moderation, and (4) Justice (Rightness) — the insistence on fairness toward all people.

Regarding the four cardinal virtues, Augustine articulated them within the context of love: "For these four virtues (would that all felt their influence in their minds as they have their names in their mouths!), I should have no hesitation

---

[145] McCloskey and Louwsma, *The Art of Virtue-based Transformational Leadership,* 46.

[146] St. Ambrose, Bishop of Milan, *Commentary of St. Ambrose on the Gospel according to St. Luke, V.* (Dublin, Ireland: Halcyon Press, 2001), 62.

in defining them: that temperance is love giving itself entirely to that which is loved; fortitude is love readily bearing all things for the sake of the loved object; justice is love serving only the loved object, and therefore ruling rightly; prudence is love distinguishing with sagacity between what hinders it and what helps it."[147]

In Christian traditions, three additional virtues were added to the four cardinal virtues of prudence, temperance, courage, and justice. These three are often referred to as theological virtues — faith, hope, and love. These three are named by Paul in 1 Corinthians 13:13, *"And now these three remain — faith, hope, and love. But the greatest of these is love."*

These seven virtues — temperance, justice, prudence, fortitude, faith, hope, and love – comprise what has come to traditionally be known as Christian virtues.

Daniel Harrington and James Keenan assert that these seven virtues can be found in who Paul was, his teachings, and by extension, the ways he led. These virtues are particularly insightful for viewing Paul as a transformational leader. Harrington and Keenan argue for seven "new virtues" to replace the "Christian virtues" arrived at in the early church.[148]

The "new virtues" that Harrington and Keenan assert can be found in Paul's life, ministry and writing are "be humble,

[147] St. Augustine of Hippo, *De morribus eccl.*, Chapter XV in *Nicene and Post-Nicene Fathers*, First Series, Vol. 4, ed. Phillip Schaff (Buffalo, NY: Christian Literature Publishing Co., 1987).
[148] Daniel Harrington and James Keenan, Paul and Virtue Ethics (Lanham, MD: Rowman and Littlefield Publishers, 2010), 125–26.

be hospitable, be merciful, be faithful, reconcile, be vigilant, and be reliable."[149]

There is a necessary movement, a renewing, and a shift in mindset that is implied in the transformational process as exemplified by Paul. His life and ministry serve as the epitome and model for what transformation looks like. He was practical and systematic, pastoral and prophetic, always seeking to live a transformed life and to lead in the transformation of others.

In summary, transformational church leadership combines spirituality — deep faith, prayer, worship, discipleship, humility, service, sacrifice, and the heart and mind of Christ (Philippians 2:4-8) — with the leadership competencies of vision, inspiring, encouraging, organizing, strategic thinking, collaboration, and team-building. For church leaders, it is not enough only to be spiritual. It is not enough to lead only out of organizational, leadership, and managerial competencies. Transformational church leaders combine both of these sets of qualities — spirituality and skills — to transform people and effect change. With this combination of spirituality and skill, leaders, churches, and communities have greater potential for vitality, thriving, and growth.

---

[149] Harrington and Keenan, Paul and Virtue Ethics, 125–26.

# CHAPTER SEVEN
## TRANSFORMED TO LEAD, PART II : PERSPECTIVES ON TRANSFORMATIONAL LEADERSHIP

*There is nothing as strong as the courage of exemplary leadership.[150]*
**Bishop Vashti McKenzie**

Critical to the future vitality of churches in the 21st-century is devising approaches to developing passionate, effective transformational leadership for ministry. Within the context of consistently rapid change, churches, like most other institutions today, need effective transformational leadership. Churches need women and men who have a vision for a better future, God's preferred future, and who possess the necessary skills to help move churches and communities toward vitality. Without transformational leadership, churches face the prospect of losing direction and failing to fulfill God's mission, vision, and purpose.

Edward Dayton and Ted Engstrom assert that there is a great need for information and guidance on leadership in not-for-profit, service, religious, and other non-business types of organizations. Not enough is known about leadership in not-for-profit organizations, given that most of the research about

---

[150] Vashti McKenzie, *Not without a Struggle: Leadership Development for African American Women in Ministry* (Cleveland, OH: United Church Press, 1996), 2.

leadership, management, and organizational theory has been concerned with profit-making organizations.[151] To remain faithful to their calling, churches have an obligation (a divine calling and mandate) to examine approaches to leadership development from multiple perspectives.

The need for effective transformational leaders is seen in the decline of many churches and denominations over the past several decades. According to Lovett Weems, "...the church has yet to explore the implications of leadership for the life of the church and the role of its leaders."[152] The church desperately needs new wisdom that draws upon the richness of Christian teaching and tradition, and, at the same time, mines the best of contemporary research on leadership.

Weems defines leadership as the channel of God's grace, and as the act of leading a group of people or an organization. In faith communities, leadership is about helping individuals discern what God is calling them to do, and helping them take their next faithful step toward God's vision.[153]

Leadership can thus also be defined as an influenced relationship between leaders and followers who seek real changes which reflect their mutual purposes. It is a process that any person can perform; it is not limited by position, title, or circumstance. It involves a set of attitudes, skills, and knowledge that are learned, not inherent, and essentially means

---

[151] Edward R. Dayton, and Ted Engstrom, *Strategy for Leadership: Planning, Activating, Motivating, Elevating* (Grand Rapids, MI: Fleming H. Revell, 1979), 14-15.

[152] Lovett H. Weems, *Church Leadership: Vision, Team, Culture and Integrity* (Nashville, Abingdon Press, 2010), xvii.

[153] Weems, *Church Leadership*, 1.

working cooperatively with others to accomplish agreed-upon goals.

The philosophies, systems, processes, and resources that need to emerge to bring about constructive approaches to leadership development for the future should be clearly defined, articulated, and developed. This could result in intentionality around leadership development, and it becoming the norm throughout churches.

Once leadership has been defined, attention can then be focused on how churches and organizations go about "channeling and tapping" into existing streams of knowledge of societal leadership and perspectives on leadership development. Then, the matter of how intentionality around nurturing and developing Christian leaders can begin to be addressed.

Weems cites David Schuller in pointing out that "the most detrimental factors in pastoral effectiveness are (1) self-serving ministry, (2) undisciplined living, and (3) emotional immaturity."[154] When any of these three appear in the behavior of the leader, ministry becomes less effective and increasingly frustrating. When the focus of the ministry is on the leader — manifesting in the appearance of a desire for affirmation, acknowledgment, control, or authority — this is when challenges in leadership can occur. When ministry and leadership are directed outwardly, when it is open, vulnerable, and charitable, is when the leader knows that they are working towards God's vision instead of their own. The need for effective leaders in the church is further articulated by Weems who quotes Letty Russell:

---

[154] Weems, *Church Leadership*, 115.

Leadership is needed for Christian communities as for other human communities, but not necessarily leadership in a fixed hierarchical model. Churches are likely to grow toward partnership among their members when there is dynamic leadership behavior among a variety of people and not just one leader.[155]

According to Peter Northouse, as its name implies, transformational leadership is a process that changes and transforms people.[156] The transformational leader's behaviors influence followers and inspire them to perform beyond their perceived abilities. As people are transformed, organizations are, by extension, transformed. The church desperately needs new wisdom that draws upon the richness of Christian teaching and tradition, and, at the same time, mines the best of contemporary research on leadership.

Northouse distinguished transactional and transformational leadership. He asserts that "In contrast to transactional leadership, transformational leadership is the process whereby a person engages with others and creates a connection that raises the level of motivation and morale in both the leader and the follower."[157] Transactional leaders develop means of exchange (quid pro quo, this-for-that, reciprocal) with followers, but the transformation of people is not necessarily

[155] Lovett Weems Jr. *Church Leadership*, xv-xvi, quoting from Letty M. Russell, *The Future of Partnership* (Philadelphia, PA: Westminster John Knox Press, 1979).

[156] Peter Northouse, *Leadership: Theory and Practice*, 8th ed. (Los Angeles: Sage Publications, Inc., 2019), 161.

[157] Northouse, *Leadership*, 164.

the primary objective of transactional leaders. In transactional leadership, behavior is maintained, and jobs are performed within the context of the static transactional relational norms that are maintained over time, like the simple expectation that people will be paid an agreed-upon salary in exchange for the work that they do. Again, this type of exchange doesn't necessarily lead to the transformation of people or organizations in the short or long term.

Northouse points out that transformational leaders set out to empower followers and nurture them in change. They attempt to raise consciousness in individuals and to get them to transcend their self-interests for the sake of others."[158]

Mark McCloskey and Jim Louwsma make further distinctions between transactional and transformational leadership. They assert that in transactional leadership, the follower serves the leader, while in transformational leadership, this is turned to where leaders serve followers and the organization.[159] They point out that the relationships of most leaders and followers are transactional, as the transactional leader seeks to make a deal, and by contrast, the transformational leader seeks to engage followers in a relationship.[160] They characterize transformational leaders as "catalysts for empowering personal change in their followers'

---

[158] Northouse, *Leadership*, 177.

[159] McCloskey and Louwsma, *The Art of Virtue-based Transformational Leadership*, 36-44.

[160] McCloskey and Louwsma, *The Art of Virtue-based Transformational Leadership*, 36-44.

lives" who hold persons accountable to "operate at their best."
[161]

Transformation can be seen through the shifting of thinking, behaviors, and habits among leaders and those being led. It implies a move from what is (actual) to a preferred state (aspirational). Based on how leadership has been defined and characterized above, then transformational leadership can be viewed as how transformation in persons is most effectively influenced by a leader or group of leaders.

McCloskey and Louwsma offer a model for virtue-based transformational leadership development, and assert that true transformation is an ongoing process that is rooted in values and mission. They state that "the leader's moral character is considered of greatest importance to a process of transformation that is driven by the values and vision of all involved...Virtue is moral strength placed in service of others."
[162]

Charles Bugg proposes that leaders must look intrinsically before seeking to motivate and lead others.[163] He asserts that it helps leaders to address the following questions: "What does God see in (me) that needs changing to become a better leader?" and "What am (I) willing to change to become a more effective, God-led leader?" He asserts that transformational leadership presumes that leaders need to change. Leadership does not mean that every one of us does

---

[161] McCloskey and Louwsma, *The Art of Virtue-based Transformational Leadership*, 20.

[162] McCloskey and Louwsma, *The Art of Virtue-based Transformational Leadership*, 45.

[163] Charles Bugg, *Transformational Leadership: Leading with Integrity* (Macon, GA: Smyth and Helwys Publishers, 2010), 5-15.

everything right or that we must be successful in each aspect of our work. Leadership not only demands risk, but it also requires a willingness to learn from mistakes and to forgive ourselves for being humans who sometimes fail God, ourselves, and others.[164]

A key issue in enacting transformational leadership models is one of awareness of where the leader is in the process, on a continuum, of moving from transactional to more transformational approaches to leadership. McCloskey and Louwsma assert that this is a process that is rooted in virtue, where the leader finds themself somewhere on a continuum, and seeks to grow into becoming more transformational, and less transactional in their leadership over time.

A final key insight from McCloskey and Louwsma regarding transformational leadership pertains to the employment of the 4-Rs model — *Relationships, Roles, Responsibilities, and Results.*[165] The 4-Rs can serve as key points of inquiry in leadership development in helping leaders better understand the impact of relationships, roles, responsibilities, and results on their overall effectiveness as leaders, along with the effectiveness of their respective teams and organizations.[166]

Using the 4-Rs as points of inquiry and qualitative assessment in leadership development can also help organizations engage more systematically and intentionally in processes of qualitatively assessing and measuring (and in some

---

[164] Bugg, *Transformational Leadership*, 13.

[165] McCloskey and Louwsma, *The Art of Virtue-based Transformational Leadership*, 36-44.

[166] McCloskey and Louwsma, *The Art of Virtue-based Transformational Leadership*, 36-44.

cases, empirically quantifying) leadership effectiveness across an organization.

Warren Bennis and Robert Thomas, in their article, "The Crucibles of Leadership", address the matters of what makes a leader, and why certain people seem to naturally inspire confidence, loyalty, and hard work, while others stumble, again and again. They assert that extraordinary leaders find meaning in — and learn from — the most negative events, and like phoenixes rising from the ashes, they emerge from adversity stronger, more confident in themselves and their purpose, and more committed to their work.[167]

Bennis and Thomas call these transformative events "crucibles" — severe tests or trials. They offer case studies of persons who have experienced "crucibles", and what can be gleaned from their experiences that give insight into what makes extraordinary, transformational leaders.

By recognizing that leadership is a group function to which all members can contribute, a sense of teamwork can be developed. Sharing leadership, recognition, satisfaction, and responsibility ensures that all the resources and skills of the group and group members will be used productively.

It is difficult for many Christian leaders to be authentically vulnerable, open, and loving in a utilitarian, materialistic, reciprocal, upwardly mobile culture that measures the value of a person by standards of productivity and efficiency. Indeed, ministry today often seems to lack the "meaningful, concrete" measures of success that our post-

---

[167] Warren Bennis and Robert Thomas, "The Crucibles of Leadership", in *HBR's 10 Must Reads on Leadership* (Boston, MA: Harvard Business Review Press, 2011), 97-114.

industrial age urgently demands. How is healing amidst personal loss and frailty, comforting and caring amidst grief, the filling of emotional emptiness, or the restoration of relationships to be measured in terms of "success" in culturally defined terms?

Henri Nouwen, in *In the Name of Jesus: Reflections on Christian Leadership,* asserted that for Christian leaders to be effective and authentic, they must address the temptations inherent in secular ideas of leadership and success while moving toward a more Christ-centered vision and practice of leadership. Nouwen further asserted that Christian leaders should consider temptations in light of the tasks and the disciplines of their calling. He addressed the temptations that all leaders feel to be relevant and essential by "[doing] things, [showing] things, [proving] things, and [building] things."[168]

He suggested that the way Christian leaders must measure the effectiveness of ministry is through their irrelevance. Just as Jesus instructed his disciples to be in the world but not of it, Nouwen said that contemporary Christian leaders must "dare to claim their irrelevance... as a divine vocation that allows them to enter into a deep solidarity with the anguish underlying all the glitter of success, and to bring the light of Christ there."[169]

This is accomplished by responding to Jesus' question to Peter on the shore of the Sea of Galilee: *"Do you love me?"* Nouwen called this question "central to all our Christian ministry...that can allow us to be, at the same time, irrelevant

---

[168] Henri J. M. Nouwen, *In the Name of Jesus: Reflections on Christian Leadership* (New York: The Crossroad Publishing Co., 2002), 28.
[169] Nouwen, *In the Name of Jesus*, 35.

and truly confident."[170] It makes us irrelevant because it redirects our attention away from the worldly demand for power, accomplishment, and control toward a loving relationship with God in Christ.

The Christian leader's irrelevance should, thus, be grounded in adherence to and operation from a completely different standard of success than that which is embraced by the world at large. The Christian leader's confidence should be grounded in knowing that sustenance comes from the power and love of God that is unconditional, without limits, and which will persevere and endure against *"all rule and authority, power and dominion"* (Ephesians 1:21).

The Christian leader can only achieve intentional irrelevance in ministry if he/she maintains and nurtures a personal relationship with God through prayer. "The central question is," Nouwen wrote, "Are leaders of the future truly men and women of God, people with an ardent desire to dwell in God's presence, to listen to God's voice, to look at God's beauty, to touch God's incarnate Word, and to taste fully God's infinite goodness?"[171]

From the church's perspective, leadership can and should offer a counter-cultural perspective to the siren calls of the modern marketplace. Church leadership - spiritual leadership - points the way to a better world, the kind of world intended by God at the dawn of creation and reiterated by Jesus in his teachings about the kingdom of God.

---

[170] Nouwen, *In the Name of Jesus*, 36.
[171] Nouwen, *In the Name of Jesus*, 43.

Effective transformational leadership helps the church understand that it does not exist in and for itself, but that it exists to be in mission and ministry with God's people.

# CHAPTER EIGHT
## TRANSFORMED TO LEAD, PART III: PERSPECTIVES ON LEADING THROUGH CHANGE

*The entrepreneur always searches for change, responds to it, and exploits it as an opportunity.*
**Peter Drucker**

In *Leadership Directions from Moses,* Olu Brown shares principles from the story of Moses to help guide leaders through challenging situations they will face. Throughout the book, Brown addresses how leaders can move forward amid difficulty.[172] He cites Moses's experiences in Numbers 32 in leading the children of Israel from bondage to freedom. Suddenly a well-planned trip threatened to veer drastically off course as two of the tribes of Israel, the Reubenites and the Gadites, ask for permission to stay in the wilderness.[173]

Moses questioned whether they were trying to avoid battles; indeed, he considered them, *"a brood of sinners"* (Num. 32:14) who repeat the unfaithfulness exhibited by the spies, the effects of which he rehearses, and which could now recur with more disastrous consequences - the destruction of Israel.[174] Like Moses, leaders today may experience

---

[172] Olu Brown, *Leadership Directions from Moses: On the Way to a Promised Land* (Nashville, TN: Abingdon Press, 2017), Brown addresses the matter of how to lead through disruption throughout the book.
[173] Brown, *Leadership Directions from Moses*, x-xi.
[174] John Bartman and John Muddiman, eds., *Oxford Bible Commentary* (Oxford, UK: Oxford University Press, 2001), 132.

"derailments" in the plans that God has given, and that they have for leading people into the future.

The effects of the COVID-19 pandemic and associated pandemonium from early 2020 into late 2022 — which are especially pronounced and evident in much of the urban space I work in as a pastor, seminary professor, leadership coach, and consultant in Baltimore, MD., and Washington, DC have seemed to take over much of our daily reality, and have resulted in more than gentle pivots in the ways that we view and understand our communities, use space and technology, and allocate resources.

I recently heard something that led me to think more deeply about the leadership that's required in crises like the pandemic and the pandemonium we've experienced. More than being able to lead organizations through a pivot or multiple pivots into "a new normal", crisis leadership today requires the ability to help organizations — systems and people — engage in pirouettes — to turn completely around, and move forward with renewed focus, energy, and purpose into "next normals". The pirouette is beautiful in the movement and balance that is required by the dancer throughout.

I've become enamored with the possibilities and opportunities for the transformation of people, places, and processes embedded in change. The vivid images of the changing colors of autumn — as is seen clearly in the color changes of leaves from summer green to beautiful, deep tones of red and orange in autumn — show the beauty that change can bring.

These necessary shifts are more like pirouettes and complete turnarounds in the ways that we must now function. With the church that I pastor (Epworth Chapel in Baltimore), the group of Baltimore parish churches and pastors that I supervise (Beloved Community Cooperative Parish, also in Baltimore), the urban churches and leaders in Wilmington, Delaware that I coach as a part of Wesley Theological Seminary's Source Collaborative, and the seminarians that teach urban ministry and community engagement in Baltimore and Washington, DC, I sense a growing openness to change and willingness to engage in pirouettes — radical shifts and turnaround - for the sake of future vitality of ministries and communities.

Peter Drucker's five questions of strategic leadership can be seen as important in helping churches move through change:

(1) What is our mission?
(2) Who is our customer (audience)?
(3) What does our customer value?
(4) What are our results?
(5) What is our plan?[175]

In *The Joy of the Gospel*, Pope Francis writes of the ways that change is incumbent in cities:

New cultures are constantly being born in these vast new expanses where Christians are no longer the customary interpreters or generators of meaning. Instead, they take from these cultures new languages, symbols, messages, and paradigms that propose new approaches to life, approaches often in contrast with the Gospel of

---

[175] Peter Drucker, *The Five Most Important Questions You Will Ever Ask About Your Organization* (San Francisco: Jossey-Bass, 1993), 11-76.

Jesus. A completely new culture has come to life
and continues to grow in the cities.[176]

Change is the process of the shifting dynamics of people
and processes within an organization or system. It can
transform us to new levels of thinking, believing, and
understanding. All people deal with change differently and
change can be brought on by many different factors. People
may resist, embrace, run away from, seek out, and/or facilitate
change. It can derive from many different sources such as loss,
separation, relocation, a change in a relationship(s), a change in
direction, a change in health, and/or personal growth. Change
has many faces.

Change is a natural phenomenon in churches and
communities, and any church that is not transforming, within
the context of the changes occurring in its ministry setting and
broader society, is on a path to decline and eventual death.
Transformation in the church, as is the case with any
organization, is driven by the quality of its leadership. This is
to say that transformational church leaders are a key
determinant in transforming churches and ministries.

Lovett Weems asserts that leadership is about change. It
is important to remember that we cannot become what we need
to be by remaining what we are.[177] A prayer from the African
American church puts it well: "Lord, we're not what we want
to be, we're not what we need to be, we're not what we are
going to be, but thank God Almighty, we're not what we used

---

[176] Pope Francis, *The Joy of the Gospel (Evangelii Gaudium)* (Washington,
DC: U.S. Office of Catholic Bishops, 2007), 38.
[177] Weems, *Church Leadership,* 22.

to be."[178] Weems provides insight into how transformational leaders help build their church's identity and facilitate vitality. He asserts that change, though difficult, is possible and that transformational leaders become skilled at facilitating organizational change and vitality.[179]

Effective transformational leaders in any context can adapt their leadership within the context that they are leading. As every leader and church needs transformation, leaders need to understand culture and context and understand the skills that are necessary to effectively lead in a particular context.

In his article, "What Leaders Really Do," John Kotter asserts that leadership and management are two distinctive and complementary systems of action. Each has its function and characteristic activities. Both are necessary for success in an increasingly complex (organizational) environment.[180] Kotter further asserts that leadership is essentially about coping with change, in contrast to management, which is about coping with complexity. Leadership is about aligning people, whereas management is about organizing systems.[181]

In *Building the Bridge as You Walk on It: A Guide to Leading Change,* Robert Quinn offers an image of leading change as one of building a bridge as it is being walked on and he posits that there's a fundamental need for leaders to be changed from within to most effectively provide transformational leadership with others. He discusses the myth

---

[178] Weems, *Church Leadership,* 22.

[179] Lovett, H., Weems, Jr., *Take the Next Step: Leading Lasting Change in the Church* (Nashville, TN: Abingdon, 2003), 17.

[180] John P. Kotter, "What Leaders Really Do", in *HBR's 10 Must Reads on Leadership* (Boston, MA: Harvard Business Review Press, 2011), 37-56.

[181] Kotter, "What Leaders Really Do", 37.

of the ruthless hero and talks about leaders who sacrifice themselves by neglecting their lives outside the job and how they are externally driven and internally closed off.

Quinn offers eight practices for entering the fundamental state of leadership, or what might also be deemed to be the journey toward transformational leadership[182]: (1) *Reflective Action* — The challenge is to be both reflective and active. This is done as the leader regularly reflects on what is happening in their life, and their leadership context. This causes leaders to constantly ask how change can occur within the leader to improve relationships and situations. (2) *Authentic Engagement* — Here, the leader is engaged in the world and acting out of who they are as their true selves, with love for what they are doing, and being authentically engaged with others. (3) *Appreciative Inquiry* — This involves a form of analysis that helps to identify and celebrate successes of the past, and move individuals and organizations toward transformation amidst rapid change. (4) *Grounded Vision* — This involves looking towards a preferred future, while also being grounded in the present reality of the people, and the facts of people's and organization's current situation. (5) *Adaptive Confidence* — Here, the leader is willing to enter uncertain situations because they have confidence in their abilities and belief in a higher purpose. The leader is confident that they can learn and adapt as they move forward. (6) *Detached Interdependence* — Here, the leader affirms the value and importance of interdependence as a means of accomplishing a mission, realizing a vision, and fulfilling a purpose. This changes perspective, and helps with focusing on collaboration

---

[182] Robert Quinn, *Building the Bridge as You Walk on It: A Guide to Leading Change* (San Francisco; Jossey-Bass, 2004), 95-184.

and the higher collective good. (7) *Responsible Freedom* —
This involves living in personal freedom and being willing to
take responsibility for one's thoughts, actions, decisions,
successes, and setbacks. (8) *Tough Love* — Here, the leader
functions as authoritative, but is humble enough to show that
they care about those they are leading and about their
organization's success.

Jesus referred to the principle of tough love as being as
wise as a serpent and as gentle as a dove (Matthew 10:17), and
Martin Luther King, Jr. spoke of this as having "a tough mind
and a tender heart."[183]

For spiritual leaders, developing the capacity to walk
through areas of uncertainty with confidence and vision and to
"build the bridge as it is being walked on" effectively means
walking by faith. An image that emerges when thinking of
"building the bridge as it is being walked on" is when Jesus
walked on water, and when Peter said, *"tell me to come to you
on the water"* (Matt. 14:22-33). Peter essentially had to walk
out in uncertainty, trusting in Jesus and although his faith was
not strong, in no small way, Peter began to build his bridge to
becoming the leader Jesus wanted him to become as he walked
on water toward Jesus.

There is evidence that points to why certain
organizations thrive amid uncertainty and change, while others
may not. Jim Collins and Morten Hansen's findings of 10x
companies (and their leaders) indicate that companies that
thrive amid uncertainty and change have an invariant
possession of the three core behaviors of *fanatic discipline,
empirical creativity,* and *productive paranoia.* These fit with

---

[183] Martin Luther King, Jr., "A Tough Mind and a Tender Heart" in *Strength
to Love* (Philadelphia, PA: Fortress Press, 1963), 13-20.

the correlative characteristics of capable, transformational leaders – *focus, collaboration, and stability*.[184] Collins and Hansen assert that these three characteristics are critical for leadership amid uncertainty and change.

Ken Cochrum's outline of *Vision, Understanding, Clarity, and Agility* (VUCA) prime skills among leaders across organizations is also helpful in understanding and leading through change. Here, attention is given to shifts in addressing *volatility, uncertainty, complexity, and ambiguity* toward a focus on *vision, understanding, clarity, and agility*. According to Cochrum, the development and deployment of these four VUCA prime skills lend to means of developing informal networks that can lead to sustainable and scalable growth across an organization. With change leadership, both people and tasks are important – and change leaders need to be both relational and missional, as was Jesus (John 13-17).[185]

In *Leading Change,* Kotter reflects on the nature of transformational leadership through organizational change and explores various dimensions of change, and how to lead through it. His eight-step change-management process involves: (1) establishing a sense of urgency, (2) creating a coalition; (3) forming a strategic vision and initiative, (4) enlisting a volunteer army, (5) enabling action by removing barriers, (6) generating short-term wins, (7) sustaining acceleration, and (8) instituting change. While Kotter's model is helpful, there needs to be room for adjustment and flexibility

---

[184] Jim Collins and Morten Hansen, *Great by Choice: Chaos, Uncertainty, and Luck* (New York: Harper Business, 2011), 3-21.
[185] Ken Cochrum, Lecture on VUCA skills in ML-923DEP-30 Fall 2020 Transformational Ministry Leadership: Theory and Practice, Bethel Theological Seminary, St. Paul, MN, Summer 2020.

in leading an organization through change. This speaks to the messiness and uncertainty embedded in change and change leadership.[186]

Kotter further asserts that today's leadership climates and change cycles are more dynamic, non-linear, and fast-paced than those of the past and often require a degree of informal networking among leaders to get things done. So, the issue revolves around how - given the volatility, uncertainty, complexity, and ambiguity embedded in change (as Cochrum proposes) — to employ Kotter's eight-step process in dynamic and fast-paced change cycles. In many respects, Kotter's eight principles - *create, build, form, enlist, enable, generate, sustain, and institute* — are not fixed in such a dual operating system but are to be constantly evaluated and tweaked in the dynamic integration of hierarchies and informal networks.

In *Resurgence: Navigating the Changing Ministry Landscape*, Candace Lewis and Rodney Smothers offer insights into ways that leaders can help churches reinvent themselves to engage their communities in new ways amid change. They state that resurgence is the next season of transformation the church can experience. It is the identification of a new skill set called "navigating" that will help in discovering best practices and new pathways that create new life in once-vital congregations.[187] Lewis and Smothers outline seven ways that "resurgence" can occur in churches as leaders facilitate the movement from *industrial to digital, comfort and care to chaos*

---

[186] John Kotter, *Leading Change* (Boston, MA: Harvard Business School, 1996), 37-168.

[187] Candace M. Lewis and Rodney Thomas Smothers, *Resurgence: Navigating the Changing Ministry Landscape* (Nashville, TN: Heritage Publishing, 2018), 10.

*and crisis, caretaker to a catalyst for change, boss to team leader, telling to coaching, scarcity to abundance, and membership to discipleship.*[188] At the heart of resurgence is transformation. Doing church differently at every level requires moving God's people to invest in a greater vision of holistic transformation.[189] This type of navigating and resurgence is critical for leaders and churches amidst and in the aftermath of the COVID-19 pandemic.

In the 1940s, Kurt Lewin developed a three-step model for leading change that can also be helpful today. Lewin's model entails *unfreezing, implementing change, and refreezing.*[190] First, leaders need to facilitate processes that help to *unfreeze* the current state and practices of the organization and convince employees and stakeholders that change is necessary. Second, it is important to *implement change* in strategic ways. And third, it is important to *refreeze* where change has been implemented and to consistently reinforce and embed change across the organization. Importantly, change leaders essentially become the chief visionaries of their organization, and must be able to clearly and consistently communicate the need for change in compelling and convincing ways, and then draw others into the process of facilitating and implementing change.

Lee Bolman and Terrance Deal's model for framing/reframing organizations (in the areas of structure, people, politics, and symbols) is also insightful for leading

---

[188] Lewis and Smothers, *Resurgence,* 45-144.

[189] Lewis and Smothers, *Resurgence*, 148.

[190] Kurt Lewin, *Field Theory in Social Science* (New York: Harper and Row, 1947). Lewin's three-step change-management model was developed in the 1940s.

change.[191] Bolman and Deal write of first being attentive to framing around structure and the importance of getting organized. In terms of human resource (people) framing, they assert, "Our most important asset is our people." Bolman and Deal also point to the complexity of understanding human needs, and the importance of other-centered communication. Understanding human needs and motivation are important considerations in any organizational setting, in seeking to maximize the effectiveness of human resources (staff and volunteers/members) who are critical to the fulfillment of the organizational mission, vision, and purpose. Bolman and Deal's outline for human resource framing points to the importance of hiring the right people, keeping them, investing in them (equipping them), empowering them, and promoting diversity (across the various forms of diversity in an organization).[192]

Bolman and Deal point out that understanding the political frame in an organization, and working to transform it where necessary, is often as daunting as it is critical, and can be important in leading change where necessary. Every organization is a "political" system within itself, with established boundaries, leadership structure (formal and informal), networks, and ways of operating. They point to the sources of power in an organization — position/authority, control of reward, coercion, information and expertise, reputation, alliance/networks, access and control of agendas, framing, and personal power (charisma).[193] These are often at

---

[191] Lee G. Bolman and Terrance Deal, *Reframing Organizations: Artistry, Choice and Leadership*, 6th ed. (San Francisco: Jossey-Bass, 2017), 3-24.
[192] Bolman and Deal, *Reframing Organizations*, 138.
[193] Bolman and Deal, *Reframing Organizations*, 192.

work simultaneously (in some ways) within an organization, and may need to be reframed to facilitate change.

A key leadership task is doing power analysis, knowing how and where power is being exerted across the organization, and by whom, and then using effective relational and other-centered communications (listening) practices, and informal networks to reframe power dynamics in ways that are most helpful to the organization.

A question that emerges is what are some of the things that serve as obstacles to addressing change? Several things that can be identified are (1) traditions, (2) habits, (3) comfort, (4) values, (5) beliefs, and (5) myopic vision. Bill Easum, in *Unfreezing Moves,* offers insight on how to unfreeze leadership and the church. He asserts that there are two kinds of churches – those that are stuck and frozen, and those that are unstuck and unfrozen.[194]

According to Easum, stuck/frozen churches are: (1) stagnant, (2) irrelevant, (3) resistant to change, (4) more interested in institutional maintenance, than fulfilling God's mission, and (5) tend to have top-down, controlling leadership structures. Characteristics of unstuck/unfrozen churches are: (1) they are permission-giving, (2) people are encouraged to discover, try, and live out their God-given gifts, (3) they equip people for ministry through developing them, (4) they tend to be team-focused, and less top-down, and (5) they are comfortable being out of control at times, and willing to learn from mistakes.

---

[194] Bill Easum, *Unfreezing Moves: Following Jesus into the Mission Field* (Nashville: Abingdon Press, 2002), 10.

Transformation and adaptation are primary challenges for the 21ˢᵗ-century church and its leaders. Given the multifarious complexities of the church and society today, leaders are challenged to lead in changing the realities in churches and communities in ways that lead to transformation. It is the transformed, transforming, transformational leader's task to speak the truth when necessary and lead change and transformation where there is un-health and dis-ease in the church and world, and to celebrate and build on those places and spaces where the church and God's people are healthy, vital, thriving, and growing, and where God's presence can be seen and felt.

# CHAPTER NINE
## HOPE FOR THE CITY: THE CASE FOR TRANSFORMATIONAL LEADERSHIP DEVELOPMENT IN URBAN MINISTRY CONTEXTS

*Technical problems can only be resolved through the application of authoritative expertise and through the organization's current structures, procedures, and ways of doing things. Adaptive problem changes can only be addressed through changes in people's priorities, beliefs, habits, and loyalties.*

*--Ronald Heifetz, Alexander Grashow, and Marty Linsky*
*The Practice of Adaptive Leadership*

The work throughout this volume is rooted in several assumptions. The first assumption is that the Bible and theology are the sources of wisdom and guidance for understanding urban contexts and informing transformational leadership development in churches in contemporary contexts. The second assumption is that persons in urban ministry contexts have gifts that can be developed for congregational effectiveness, vitality, and growth. The third assumption is that the local church is an essential agent of God's plan and mission in developing transformational leaders. The fourth assumption is that churches can and should implement strategies for identifying, nurturing, and developing transformational leadership. And the fifth assumption is that transformational leadership development is a holistic and ongoing process.

Several questions have served as the impetus for the volume: (1) How might transformational leadership be developed, then multiplied/replicated among those who are being led? (2) As it regards results, what is a healthy balance between spiritual transformation/renewal and physical/material/empirical evidence of transformation? (3) How can transformational leadership be developed, sustained, and scaled in individuals and communities over time?

Several observations can be made about urban ministry and transformational leadership. Among these observations are: (1) the leadership of the biblical figures Nehemiah and Paul serve as models of exemplary transformational leadership; (2) there are unique characteristics of ministry in urban contexts, and thus the need for unique approaches to performing ministry in these contexts; (3) some of the unique qualities that can be identified in effective urban ministry practitioners like adaptability, rationality, collaboration, creativity, resourcefulness, and persistence are helpful for transformational leaders; and (4) relationships and adaptability play central roles in transformational leadership. The evidence in the works discussed earlier in this volume on leadership and change by Lovett Weems, Robert Quinn, John Kotter, Jim Collins, and others points to transformational leadership being closely connected to relationality and adaptability in leaders; and (5) transformational leadership is essential to transforming people and organizations and is critical for organizational thriving.

The biblical foundations for this volume are based on the Book of Nehemiah and Paul's life and writings. The

Nehemiah text and Pauline writings show that both Nehemiah and Paul possessed significant transformational leadership qualities that inform how transformational leadership is carried out in churches today. Scripture informs the work of transformed and transforming leadership in Romans 12:2, as Paul encouraged persons to *"be not conformed to the world, but be transformed by the renewing of (your) minds."* Paul follows this by writing in Romans 12:8, *"If your gift is to lead, do it diligently."*

A theological foundation of this volume is found in ways that the Trinity is an expression of the lived theology of collaboration, and valuing the gifts of all persons. In Ephesians 4:11-13, the apostle Paul points to the diversity of gifts that are found in the body of Christ:

> So, Christ himself gave the apostles, the prophets, the evangelists, the pastors and teachers, to equip his people for works of service, so that the body of Christ may be built up until we all reach unity in the faith and the knowledge of the Son of God and become mature, attaining to the whole measure of the fullness of Christ.

Again, Paul's encouragement in Romans 12:2 is most applicable, where he encouraged believers to *"be not conformed to the world, but be transformed by the renewing of your mind."* This points to where the transformation of leaders can begin, and where breakthroughs are possible with the renewing of the minds of leaders. This is to say that it is important that processes be enacted where leaders can be transformed to lead in transformational ways. This is essentially what happened with leaders like Nehemiah and Paul, which ultimately resulted in the impact that both had as transformational leaders in their respective ministry contexts.

Every leader and church needs transformation. Any church that is not transforming, within the context of the changes occurring in its ministry context and community, is on a path to decline and death. Transformation in the church, as is the case with any organization, is driven by the quality of its leadership. This is to say that transformed church leaders are a key determinant in transforming churches and ministries. Transformational leaders lead in transforming churches.

There is a need for transformational leadership development training specifically designed for leaders (clergy and laity) serving in urban ministry contexts. In their book, *The Practice of Adaptive Leadership: Tools and Tactics for Changing Your Organization and the World*, Ronald Heifetz, Alexander Grashow, and Marty Linsky suggest that two types of problems impact organizational change. The first is a technical problem, where current knowledge can be applied to resolve the concern. The second is an adaptive problem, where new behaviors must be adopted to resolve the issue. Technical problems can be resolved through the application of authoritative expertise and through the organization's current structures, procedures, and ways of doing things. Adaptive problems can only be addressed through changes in people's priorities, beliefs, habits, and loyalties.[195] This volume addresses the adaptive problem of a need for transformational leadership development processes and models for leaders serving in urban ministry contexts.

---

[195] Ronald Heifetz, Alexander Grashow, and Marty Linsky, *The Practice of Adaptive Leadership: Tools and Tactics for Changing Your Organization and the World* (Boston, MA: Harvard Business Press, 2009), 69-89.

# CHAPTER TEN
## HOPE FOR THE CITY : SEVEN AXIOMS FOR TRANSFORMATIONAL LEADERSHIP DEVELOPMENT IN URBAN MINISTRY CONTEXTS

In light of data collected through case studies that I have conducted on several urban churches in Baltimore, MD., Washington, DC, Wilmington, DE., and Birmingham, AL., and several other cities across the United States over the past several years, and in light on over 50 one-on-one interviews and several focus groups I have conducted with numerous church and community leaders (lay and clergy), several axioms have been identified as foundational to developing processes and models for transformational leadership development for persons serving in urban ministry settings. It is intended that the seven axioms that follow could serve as the foundation of processes and models for transformational leadership development for persons serving and leading in urban ministry contexts.

***Axiom One: Understand the Unique Qualities of Urban Contexts and Urban Ministry***

Leaders in urban ministry settings must understand the unique nature of the urban context, and by extension, the unique nature of urban ministry. In *The Joy of the Gospel (Evangelii Gaudium),* Pope Francis writes of challenges in urban cultures. He intimates:

The New Jerusalem, the holy city (cf. Rev. 21:2-4), is the goal toward which all of humanity is moving. Curiously, God's revelation tells us that the fullness of humanity and history is realized in a city. We need to look at our cities with a contemplative gaze, a gaze of faith that sees God as dwelling in their homes, in their streets and squares.[196]

Pope Francis further intimates:

In cities, as opposed to the countryside, the religious dimension of life is expressed in different lifestyles and daily rhythms linked to places and people. In their daily lives, people must often struggle for survival, and this struggle contains within it a profound understanding of life which often includes a deep religious sense.[197]

As was shared earlier in this volume, according to Ronald Peters, urban ministry is a way of understanding God, based on the dynamics of the city, and involves a theological praxis that seeks to enhance the quality of life for all creation.[198] Peters asserts that particular core values are incumbent in approaches to doing ministry in urban contexts. He states that core values are "those ideals or principles that form the essence of Christian ministry. They are basic, central, nonnegotiable beliefs that motivate and energize ministry." Another definition of a core value is that it is a "principle that guides the

---

[196] Pope Francis, *The Joy of the Gospel*, 37.
[197] Pope, Francis, *The Joy of the Gospel,* 37.
[198] Peters, *Urban Ministry,* 8.

organization's internal conduct and its relationship with the external world."

According to Lovett Weems, core values speak to congregational identity (who we are). Values describe the commitments of any organization that shapes the way that organization does its work. If the mission defines what the organization will do, values describe the commitments that will be honored in the fulfillment of the mission.[199]

As is the case in any organization, a church's ability to develop, articulate, and implement its core values is critical to fulfilling its mission, vision, and purpose (MVP). **Core values essentially speak to:**

1. *Identity.* Who a church believes it is.
2. *Theology.* How a church believes it fits with God's vision for it.
3. *Action.* How a church will act on what it says it believes.

Identifying a clear set of core values is essential for guiding ministry in urban contexts. Peters states that core values undergird the self-esteem and vision of individuals and the church as a community. With them, the gospel can become a reality in the lives of people.[200] He identifies six core values that are essential for urban ministry: *theism, love, community, creativity, reconciliation, and hope.*[201]

As a church plans to engage in ministry, its core values are a key mechanism for keeping it focused and on track, and

---

[199] Weems, *Church Leadership*, 33.
[200] Peters, *Urban Ministry*, 110.
[201] Peters, *Urban Ministry*, 112-134.

they are essential to connecting the church's mission to the specific needs and opportunities of its community. In a planning process, they provide a reflective mechanism for the development of church-wide goals and objectives. They can be used to determine whether a new ministry opportunity fits the church's values. And they help individual church members live out their lives as Christ-followers.

In light of this, a church needs to identify its core values in the context of its specific community. A church that effectively identifies, develops, articulates, and appropriates its core values can remain clear on what it believes about itself, and focused on what God calls it to be and do. The church can then implement its mission, vision, and purpose (MVP) statements with careful consideration of its core values and can give careful consideration to new opportunities for church and community engagement that align with the core values. For instance, churches might develop partnerships with community entities like schools as these ministry opportunities fit the church's core values. A church that effectively develops, articulates and appropriates its core values can remain clear on what it believes about itself (who it is), and focused on what God calls it to be and do (what it will do).

### *A Case in Point: Epworth Chapel, Baltimore*

As Epworth Chapel, Baltimore has engaged in strategic planning processes over the past several years and sought to devise strategies and approaches to more effectively engage its urban context, the church has spent a considerable amount of time in discernment, clarifying its core values in light of its history, present realities, and hope for the future. Epworth

Chapel's strategic plan states that: *"As a church, our values stand at the core of all that we are, all that we do, and all that we seek to become as the people of God."* The seven core values that Epworth Chapel has adopted are:

1. *Prayer.* Public, private, and communal prayer is central to all that we do.
2. *Excellence.* We strive to offer God and one another our best in all that we do.
3. *Hospitality.* Everyone we encounter should receive radical hospitality, and a friendly and open welcome and all persons are to be treated as full participants in the body of Christ.
4. *Justice.* We are committed to a vision of a society where every individual has equal access to the resources, opportunities, benefits, and protections that society offers, and where every individual is treated with dignity and fairness.
5. *Family-focused.* We affirm and support the building of strong families as we model what it means to be the family of God.
6. *Nurturing.* We are committed to supporting and encouraging each other and providing opportunities for all persons to grow as disciples of Jesus Christ.
7. *Diversity.* We believe that there is strength in welcoming and accepting persons of all ages, genders, races, abilities, orientations, identities, and nationalities — all God's people — into the church family.

These seven stated core values serve as guides for the ongoing ministry planning and implementation processes at Epworth Chapel in the church and serve as reflective lenses as the church establishes the annual goals and objectives that it seeks to accomplish as it seeks to live out its mission, vision, and purpose and impact its community.

## *Axiom Two: Understand and Organize the Church in Relationship with its Community*

The Christian church is the means through which the ministry of Jesus Christ as the kingdom of God is continuously carried forth into the world. Through its various means of serving the world, the church is the redemptive bridge between God and humanity. It is God working in and through persons, as God continues, through Christ, to reconcile the world unto Godself. As Paul intimated, *"God was in Christ reconciling the world to Godself"* (2 Corinthians 5:17-18).

As the Body of Christ, the church serves as an integrative bridge across the divides of the many societal entities with which it relates. Given the growing diversity in many urban contexts, one predominant issue remains how to facilitate common ground among persons from different cultural, socioeconomic, political, racial, and religious backgrounds.

In the church's quest to become the emblem of community — as Christ existing as community — it must endeavor to model the ministry of Christ — a ministry of unconditional love, compassion, justice, redemption, and reconciliation — through which Jesus sought to address the particular spiritual and social concerns among those whom he encountered in his ministry context, which was primarily in Nazareth and Galilee — an urban ministry context.

In his video presentation, "Why Community Engagement Matters" Lovett Weems Jr. states "…the longer a church exists the less knowledgeable it tends to be about its community and the less connected it is with its community…"[202] Weems' assessment seems to apply regarding the challenges of many churches to adapt to and engage the changes in their respective communities.

Kimberly Bobo, in her article "Church Involvement in Community Organizations", asserts that "Although churches have always been the heart of community life, they haven't always worked closely with other denominational or faith bodies, let alone with other institutions in the community.[203]

Religious leaders can play important roles in enacting changes to improve social, economic, and political conditions in communities. In *Faith after Ferguson*, Leah Gunning Francis states that "there is no doubt that pastors and preachers have an influential role in helping congregations think critically about troubling social norms or personal experiences, and offer a theological reflection on how God's presence/activity is understood in the midst of it."[204]

---

[202] Lovett H. Weems, Jr., Lewis Center Director, "Why Community Engagement Matters," Lewis Center for Church Leadership, October 26, 2018, video of lecture, accessed December 31, 2020,

[203] Kimberly Bobo, "Church Involvement in Community Organizations." *Review & Expositor* 92, no. 1 (February 1995): 31–38, accessed August 28, 2022.

[204] Leah Gunning Francis, *Faith after Ferguson: Resilient Faith in Pursuit of Racial Justice* (St. Louis, MO: Chalice Press, 2021), 144.

According to the American Journal of Public Health, a common definition of a community is that it is a group of people with diverse characteristics who are linked by social ties, share common perspectives, and engage in joint action in geographical locations or settings.[205] In the *Art of Relevance*, Nina Simon asserts that a community is a group of people who share something in common. A community can be defined by the shared attributes of the people in it and/or by the strength of the connections among them.[206]

Several sociological aspects of communities can be identified. First, a community is a group of people who interact with one another, for example, as friends or neighbors. Second, this interaction is typically viewed as occurring within a bounded geographic territory, such as a neighborhood or city. Third, the community's members often share common values, beliefs, or behaviors.

And every type of community can be classified by the purpose for which it brings people together. Some of these purposes are (1) Interest — communities of people who share the same interest or passions; (2) Action — communities of people trying to bring about change; (3) Place — communities of people brought together by geographic boundaries; (4) Practice — communities of people in the same profession or undertaking the same activities; and (5) Circumstance — communities of people brought together by external events/situations.

---

[205] *American Journal of Public Health* (Washington, DC: American Public Health Association 2001).
[206] Nina Simon, *Art of Relevance* (Santa Cruz, CA: Museum Publishing, 2016).

One objective of strengthening leaders in their service in urban ministry settings is to strengthen communities. Frank Maddison Reid, formerly the pastor of Bethel African Methodist Episcopal Church in Baltimore, MD, and now a bishop in the African Methodist Episcopal Church, asserts that as this was the case for Nehemiah, it is the case today.

We see in Nehemiah that God is giving us insight into the local church and our purpose within the church. We find that the walls of Jerusalem had been broken down before Nehemiah's day. The walls are symbolic of the fact that the family structure and the spirit of the people have been destroyed. After Nehemiah had shared with them the plan to rebuild the walls, the people said, "Let us rise and build." Next, we find that they have moved to the reality of actually building.[207]

An important function of urban churches and ministries in urban contexts is participating in processes of community engagement, organizing, and development. According to Robert Lupton, the most important aspect of community development is to listen. Becoming a neighbor versus an intruder is grounded in vulnerability. It takes time to develop relationships and to lessen power differentials. It takes time to develop the relationships to become an authentic neighbor. He explains that "the best way to assure effectiveness is to spend enough time as a learner, ask enough questions, and seek wisdom from indigenous leaders to gain an accurate picture of

---

[207] Frank Madison Reid, III, *The Nehemiah Plan: Preparing the Church to Rebuild Broken Lives* (Shippensburg, PA: Treasure House, 1993), 64.

both existing realities and future aspirations of the community."[208]

An important core practice that helps inform community organizing and engagement is to conduct community asset mapping. In asset mapping, there is a core belief that good already exists in communities. Six key asset types in most communities are (1) Physical – buildings, land, location, housing, roads; (2) Economic – banks, stores; (3) Stories – history, culture; (4) People - skills, capacity, agency, connections; (5) Associations – organizations; and (6) Institutions - schools, religious bodies.

Many urban communities are becoming more diverse racially, economically, and socially. Juana Bordas asserts that leadership in communities of color is based on a circular form where responsibility is shared and reciprocal. Building a circle of leadership empowers people, creates the critical mass needed for social change, and establishes a legacy for succeeding generations.[209]

Joy Skjegstad posits that there are at least seven creative models for community ministry (1) Donate Goods or Money (2) Mobilize Volunteers, (3) Partner with Other Organizations, (4) Advocate around Public Policy, (5) Engage in Community Organizing, (6) Develop a Ministry Program, and (7) Create a Church-based Nonprofit.[210] Many churches engage in a

---

[208] Robert Lupton, *Toxic Charity: How Churches and Charities Hurt Those They Help* (San Francisco, HarperOne, 2011), 175.

[209] Juana Bordas, *Salsa, Soul, and Spirit: Leadership for a Multicultural Age: New Approaches to Leadership from Latino, Black, and American Indian Communities,* 2nd ed. (San Francisco, CA: Berrett-Koehler, 2012), 140.

[210] Joy F. Skjegstad, *7 Creative Models for Community Ministry* (Valley Forge, PA: Judson Press, 2013), these seven models for community ministry are discussed throughout the book.

combination of several of these community ministry models based on the church's mission, vision, and purpose and the community's specific needs and opportunities.

In *Doing Justice: Congregations and Community Organizing,* Dennis Jacobsen asserts that congregation-based community organizing is rooted in the local congregation. Organizing must be linked to the faith and values of the local congregation, to its self-interest, and to the realities of the neighborhood. He offers a challenge to churches to take a hard look at their relationship with their community and to understand how churches, as part of a community, engage in the public arena. In referencing Dietrich Bonhoeffer, Jacobsen implores churches to understand that being Christian is about being for others and that "self-preservation is antithetical to the cross of Jesus Christ."[211]

In terms of faith-based community organizing, Jacobsen also calls for reflection on power dynamics, and how power is used, especially in whom it benefits. Additionally, he calls for reflection on how values are lived authentically versus in transmuted forms that benefit the status quo. In terms of power analysis, Robert Linthicum, in *Building a People of Power,* asserts that:

> This is the primary purpose of community organizing - to create out of a victimized, marginalized, destructive collection of people a community where the quality of life is such that people find fulfillment and joy in living there. The

---

[211] Dennis Jacobsen, *Doing Justice: Congregations and Community Organizing* (Minneapolis: Fortress Press, 2001), 15.

power of the oppressor must be replaced by a
quality of corporate life that is of such superiority
to either that of the formerly oppressed or their
oppressors that it brings purpose, direction, joy,
and fulfillment to all who experience it. That is the
chief end for building a people of power.[212]

According to Jacobsen, while power dynamics can
create life energy, through empowerment and building
community, they can also perpetuate oppressive structures
which suppress growth and life energy.[213] He frames a vision of
congregation-based community organizing and the shift of
power bases from oppressor-victim to one oriented around
justice, stating that faith-based community organizing "must
develop the same sweeping vision for justice that the church has
for evangelism."[214] Both have power; the former is to
evangelize and expand the message; yet, the latter is a form of
shared empowerment. The power lies in the people of God
rather than the power of a few.

### *Lessons for the church and community from the Covid-19 Pandemic*

Crisis can reveal the strength of the church's ministries
of connection with their community and their message of hope.

---

[212] Robert Linthicum, *Building a People of Power, Equipping Churches to Transform their Communities* (Federal Way, WA: World Vision, 2005), 173.
[213] Jacobsen, *Doing Justice*, 73.
[214] Jacobsen, *Doing Justice*, 73.

The circumstances of the COVID-19 pandemic presented churches and leaders with unprecedented opportunities and challenges. Churches had to discover new ways to minister through a crisis. The lessons learned will likely result in new and different ways of engaging in ministry going forward.[215] The COVID-19 pandemic also revealed the vital importance of the church's spiritual presence and the need to stay connected with one another and serve the broader community. There are several key lessons for how churches can minister and how leaders can lead amid crises.

## 1. *Ministries of prayer and presence are as important as ministries of performance and provision.*

In a crisis, there is a pronounced sense of humanity's need for and assurance of God's presence, and the church becomes a primary means of such assurance. Thus, ministries of prayer and presence, even when conducted virtually, become critical. Amidst COVID-19, some churches reported growth in their prayer ministries. Some started new virtual prayer ministries and small groups aimed at spiritual formation and congregational care.

## 2. *The church remains an essential aspect of community and connection for people of all generations.*

Crisis confirms that the church is essentially community or, as Dietrich Bonhoeffer posited over 90 years ago, "The

---

[215] C. Anthony Hunt, "Why the Church's Mission Really Matters in this Time of Crisis" in *Leading Ideas* (Washington, DC: Lewis Center for Church Leadership, June 3, 2020).

church is Christ existing as community". In times of disruption, crisis, and isolation, people yearn for ways to be connected and in community, and the church becomes a primary means of sustaining community, belonging, and meaning for many people.

### 3. The church's missional presence still matters.

Crises such as COVID-19 often result in a heightened awareness of and need for the church's missional presence in the community. This was confirmed by rising unemployment rates and other economic challenges in communities surrounding many churches due to the COVID-19 pandemic. Through the COVID-19 crisis, many churches continued to engage in vital community ministry, and some reported an expansion in such community ministries. For instance, Epworth Chapel UMC in Baltimore partnered with the Maryland Food Bank and other entities to distribute over 300,000 pounds of free fresh food to its neighborhood as the church's fellowship hall became a regional community food distribution hub.

### 4. The church can never go wrong when it preaches and practices hope amidst crisis.

Christian hope is and will continue to be the antidote and antithesis to existential despair. Martin Luther King Jr. intimated in his 1967 sermon, "The Meaning of Hope," that "hope is the refusal to give up despite overwhelming odds."[216] A half-century later, Walter Brueggemann wrote in his

---

[216] Martin Luther King, Jr., "The Meaning of Hope," (Atlanta, GA: Martin Luther King, Jr. King Center Archives), 5ff, the sermon was delivered on December 10, 1967.

book, *Gospel of Hope*, that "Hope is the deep religious conviction that God has not quit."[217] Amidst any form of crisis — personal or social — people essentially look to churches to be avenues of community-building, heralds of hope, and agents of the promise that God's future will be better than current conditions.

### *A Case in Point: St. John's United Methodist Church, Houston, Texas*

Rudy Rasmus is the pastor of St. John's United Methodist Church in downtown Houston, Texas. St. John's Church is one of the fastest-growing inner-city congregations in America, having grown from 25 active members in 1990 to over 8,000 active members today. Rasmus asserts that to have a strong, vibrant ministry in urban communities, 5-Cs must be incorporated: *common sense, collaboration, commitment, consistency, and contributions.*[218] He shares that it is important to "set clear goals and establish a workable strategy. Ask plenty of questions, build a great team, and look for resources to help you. If your heart is broken because you see the needs of men, women, boys, and girls on the street, enlist the leaders of your church to pray and help communicate God's love in a tangible way to those who desperately need it. As God leads you to build your team and find resources, take action to touch the lives of "the least of these."[219]

---

[217] Walter Brueggemann, *A Gospel of Hope* (Louisville, KY: Westminster John Knox Press, 2018), 105.

[218] Rudy Rasmus, "Leading Ministry with the Homeless" in *Leading Ideas* (Washington, DC: Lewis Center for Church Leadership, June 24, 2009).

[219] Rasmus, "Leading Ministry with the Homeless".

## *Axiom Three: Develop a Culture for Transformational Leadership in the Church/Ministry*

Effective leadership engenders hope, which in turn transforms lives, allowing people to better know God and do God's will. From a Christian perspective, leadership can and should offer a counter-cultural perspective to the siren calls of the modern marketplace. Effective leadership points the way to a better world, the kind of world that God intended at the dawn of creation and that Jesus reiterated in his teachings about the kingdom of God. Leadership helps the church understand that it does not exist for itself, but exists to be in mission and ministry with God's people.

Among numerous dimensions of leadership, this volume has offered definitions and characteristics of transformational leadership and provided a distinction between transactional and transformational leadership. Leadership expert James MacGregor Burns asserts that transformational leadership occurs when leaders and followers help each other advance to a higher level of effectiveness, morality, and motivation."[220] Burns, Peter Northouse, and other transformational leadership theorists posit that transactional and transforming leadership are mutually exclusive styles.

It is important to reiterate the distinction between transactional and transformational leadership. United Methodist Bishop William Willimon points out that the transactional leader discerns the needs of followers and

---

[220] James Macgregor Burns, *Transforming Leadership,* (New York: Grove Press, 2004), 207.

performs leadership as a set of expectations to be met, and a series of jobs to be done. Leadership is thus a transaction between the expectations of the followers and meeting those expectations by the leader. Transformative leadership seeks more than merely managing the felt needs of followers. The transformative leader elevates followers to a higher level, refusing to be either trapped or driven by conventional expectations of followers, calling followers to a higher purpose — a higher moral commitment — thus transforming the organization and its members.[221]

Burns asserts that through the strength of their vision and personality, transformational leaders can inspire followers to change expectations, perceptions, and motivations to work toward common goals. Burns also describes transformational leaders as those who can move followers up on Maslow's hierarchy, but also move them to go beyond their interests.[222]

Leadership may have as much in common with jazz music as it does with the ministry. As a fan of jazz music, I see that leadership, like jazz, requires active listening, improvisation, and a certain lack of definition. Simply asking twelve people to define leadership will likely bring a dozen different responses. When an interviewer asked the great jazz trumpeter Louis Armstrong, "What is jazz?" Armstrong famously replied, "Man, if you have to ask, you'll never know!"

Lovett Weems offers ten observations about leadership. He proposes that:

(1) leadership needs to be demythologized

---

[221] William Willimon, *Pastor: The Theology and Practice of Ordained Ministry* (Nashville, TN: Abingdon Press, 2002), 279.
[222] Burns, *Transforming Leadership*, 207-208.

(2) leadership is not simple

(3) leadership is spiritual

(4) leadership is about group process

(5) leadership is chaotic

(6) leadership is funny

(7) most research on leadership is not taking place in the church

(8) any learning about leadership is only a beginning

(9) leadership is an art

(10) leadership is never an end in itself.[223]

Weems asserts that leaders must be willing and able to relinquish their authoritative leadership role to strengthen others in the joint task of implementing the vision for the community.[224] A leader, he writes, must be "able constantly to shift roles among being leader, peer, and follower."[225] In this way, a leader empowers others to share personally in the organization's vision.

Because, by definition, the transformational leader believes in the responsibility and ability of the group members to reach decisions, they help members maintain and develop the group, while encouraging them to be more effective individual participants. A leader actively promotes the involvement of all members and sees the group as a whole, not just a collection of individuals. They should be aware of how morale, feelings, or satisfaction can change group dynamics.

Several qualities are, thus, identifiable in transformational leaders. These qualities include:

---

[223] Weems, *Church Leadership*, 13-29.

[224] Weems, *Church Leadership*, 67.

[225] Weems, *Church Leadership*, 58.

(1) *Vision* - the ability to see beyond today

(2) *Courage* - the boldness to implement a vision despite opposition, criticism, and a chance of failure

(3) *Confidence* - believing in oneself and one's goals

(4) *Humility* - confidence must be balanced with humility. One must not be so confident that he/she ignores the counsel of others

(5) *Determination* - tenacity and persistence that refuses to quit or become discouraged because of hardships, difficulties, or opposition

(6) *Energy* - is a hard worker, and realizes that hard work is a key to success

(7) *Organizational ability* - must be adept at organizing people and tasks

(8) *Follower/Team Focus* – is focused on the well-being and success of team members and the organization

(9) *Concern* - cares for group members, as much as for his/her goals

Additionally, a transformational leader will do several things: (1) They will involve everyone in building and maintaining group cohesion. People tend to support what they help to create. (2) They will view leadership as service. It is a way to help the group develop an atmosphere of trust that helps accomplish goals and objectives. (3) They will help the group see how it can deal with internal conflicts that may disrupt meetings, slow down the accomplishment of goals, or alienate group members. (4) They encourage the group to work through conflict as a group dynamic, and as a natural part of change and growth.

Finally, transformational leaders *CARE*. They (1) *Communicate* with competence their confidence in group members; (2) *Always* are available to support group members and the organization; (3) *Remember* to be responsible and responsive to group members and other stakeholders; and (4) *Energize* their group by being enthusiastic about others' ideas and efforts.

### *A Case in Point: Epworth Chapel, Baltimore*

Since 2011, Epworth Chapel UMC has developed and implemented an ongoing process of transformational leadership development which entails three components: *training, coaching, and resourcing.* The coaching aspect of this leadership development approach will be discussed in detail in Axiom Six.

This volume, *Hope for the City,* is an outcome of my doctoral research in transformational leadership at Bethel University and the Graduate Theological Foundation, and advanced study in the Executive Leadership Program at the Said Business School, University of Oxford. Additionally, this volume is an outcome of the development of several training resources (including several workshops, and leadership retreats) at Epworth Chapel designed to address the specific leadership development needs of persons serving at Epworth Chapel and in urban ministry contexts. In conversations with church and community leaders in Baltimore and other cities, the need for print and electronic media resources was identified.

In light of this, an *Urban Leadership Handbook,* which is available in print and electronic formats has also been developed. The topics covered in the handbook are:

(1) Understanding the Urban Context and Urban Ministry
(2) Understanding Transformational Leadership
(3) Developing Effective Teams
(4) Visioning
(5) Delegating Responsibility
(6) Goal-Setting/Action Planning
(7) Facilitating Change
(8) Managing Conflict
(9) Conducting Effective Meetings
(10) Dealing with Trauma and Grief
(11) Understanding Community/Asset Mapping
(12) Community Engagement and Organizing.

The *Urban Leadership Handbook* is a complement to a twelve-week transformational leadership development course that serves as the training component of this model. Topics covered in the course are:

(1) Understanding the Urban Context and Urban Ministry
(2) Understanding Transformational Leadership
(3) Building Effective Teams
(4) Leading through Change
(5) Turning Vision into Action
(6) Ministry Outside the Box (Creativity, Innovation, Media, and Community Ministry)
(7) Understanding Community

(8) Organizing for Community Change/Principles of Community Organizing

(9) Developing a Coach Approach to Developing Leaders

(10) Community Asset Mapping

(11) Resource Identification, Development and Partnerships

(12) Developing Ministry Action Plans and SMART Goals.

The intent for the use of these leadership development resources and training is that they could be used in a variety of urban ministry settings to effectively develop transformational leaders and help develop healthier churches and communities.

## *Axiom Four: Devise a Strategy for Identifying and Nurturing High-impact Leaders*

One of the key premises informing this volume is that a church that engages in careful discernment about leadership identification, nurture, and development creates a leadership climate that maximizes the use of the gifts, passion, and commitment of persons in the congregation. Over time, this process of developing high-impact leaders can result in sustained vitality and growth for the fulfillment of the church's vision, mission, and purpose.

This is to say that the development of high-impact leaders is critical to ongoing congregational effectiveness, vitality, and growth. Local church practices that identify, nurture, and develop passionate, effective leaders are a key to engendering hope, which in turn transforms lives, allowing persons to better know God and to do God's will.

## *A Case in Point: Epworth Chapel, Baltimore*

In 2014 at Epworth Chapel, we began an intentional process of discernment around high potential/impact leadership. I shared with the church's leadership team what I deemed to be the *three keys to identifying and developing high-impact leaders — gifts, passion, and commitment.*[226]

## *Three Key Questions*

Each year at Epworth Chapel, I work with the church's leadership development team on the critical task of identifying and developing persons to serve in various leadership roles across the church. Before looking at specific criteria and qualities that might qualify a particular person to serve in a specific leadership role, we ask three preliminary questions:

1. Does the person demonstrate a love of God as evidenced by active participation in the worship life of the church?
2. Does the person demonstrate a love of the local church through the sharing of their time, talent,

---

[226] C. Anthony Hunt, "Three Keys to Identify and Develop High Impact Leaders" in *Leading Ideas.* (Washington, DC: Lewis Center for Church Leadership, May 18, 2016).

and tithes (money) in service to the church and community?

3. Does the person relate to and work well with other people and demonstrate that he or she can be a team player?

If the leadership development team answers "yes" to each of these three questions, then we seek to discern whether and where a particular person might best lead in the life of Epworth Chapel. The goal is to place people in leadership roles where they can find the most fulfillment and have the most impact. Here, three matters are weighed - *gifts, passion, and commitment.*

## *Identifying Gifts*

Discernment around gifts for ministry and leadership is rooted in the premise that each of us is uniquely gifted. At Epworth Chapel, we often use spiritual gifts inventories and other gifts instruments such as StrengthsFinder® to help persons clarify their areas of giftedness. This helps define the areas where the individual might be best suited to lead in the church.

## *Identifying Passion*

After gifting has been clarified, then the leadership development team engages in discernment around passion. Here, we work from the premise that gifts for leadership alone are insufficient for the development of a high-impact leader. Gifts without passion are simply gifts. But gifts coupled with passion move persons toward actualizing and maximizing their leadership in impactful ways. Someone might be gifted in a particular area but have no passion for using those gifts as a leader in the church. For instance, a person might be a gifted school principal in their professional life but have no passion for being a Sunday school superintendent. We can't assume that a great public-school educator has the passion to lead Sunday school. In the case of this gifted educator, the church is better served if it helps this person find another area where they are gifted, perhaps in church administration, finance, or community organizing where they also have some passion for leading in the church.

### *Identifying Commitment*

Once gifting and passion for a ministry area have been determined, there is discernment around commitment. Here, again, we don't presume that everyone gifted and passionate about a particular ministry area is committed to serving to the best of their ability. Other commitments — family, professional, or recreational — can prevent gifted and passionate people from providing high-impact leadership in the church. For instance, the outstanding educator cited above, who might potentially serve well as a church council or finance chair, might be at a point in their career where they don't have the time to commit to providing such leadership in the church at this point in their life.

In summary, a church that develops high-impact leaders by discerning gifts, passion, and commitment will, over time, experience sustained vitality and growth for the church's mission into the future.

## *Axiom Five: Focus on Developing Teamwork and Collaboration*

A critical aspect of transformational leadership development is effective team-building. Teams are necessary for all organizational settings — religious, non-profit, for-profit, governmental, and educational — given the challenges that organizations face today, and given the rate at which change is occurring.

Three premises are involved as it regards developing teams. They are: (1) developing highly effective teams is critical for growth within an organization; (2) the leader plays a critical role in developing teams; and (3) there are numerous factors involved in how teams develop from when they start to the point of their maturity and high effectiveness.

### *The Importance of Developing Teams*

Teams are critical to the effectiveness of any organization. John Katzenbach and Douglas Smith assert that one critical concern is determining the difference between a team and other groups in an organization.[227] They highlight that the performance challenges that today's organizations face demand responsiveness, speed, and quality that are difficult for

---

[227] Jon R. Katzenbach and Douglas K. Smith, "The Discipline of Teams" in *HBR's 10 Must Reads on Teams* (Boston, MA: Harvard Business Review Press, 2013), 35-38.

individuals to attain when working alone.[228] The complexity
and pace of organizational change make teams necessary.
Effective leaders exert great effort in building teams. They
understand the importance of being both a leader and a servant
of the team, and they willingly acknowledge indebtedness and
gratitude to team members.

Involvement and collaboration are keys to
organizational effectiveness. Katie Carson Phillips offers six
leadership practices for enhancing committed involvement.
These practices are: knowing people, widening the circle, being
patient, taking care of people, communicating purpose, and
modeling what you believe.[229] Phillips asserts that these six
basic practices strengthen a culture of collaborative leadership
that can enable meaningful engagement.

Creating an environment for collaboration is essential
for organizational effectiveness. Jason Carthen states that
"Corporations such as Google, General Electric, and Apple
point to a healthy team-based culture that bolsters progress and
promotes shared thinking for consistent goal achievement."[230] I
have found in my work and leadership in several organizational
settings over the years - for-profit, non-profit, educational,
military, governmental, and religious - that such modeling can
be challenging, given the general tendencies of people to think
and function individually. So, to shift from individual to team-

---

[228] Jon R. Katzenbach and Douglas K. Smith, *The Wisdom of Teams: Creating the High-performance Organization* (Boston: Harvard Business Review Press, 1992), 12.
[229] Katie Carson Phillips, "6 Leadership Practices to Enhance Involvement and Collaboration" in *Leading Ideas* (Washington, DC, Lewis Center for Church Leadership, March 2020).
[230] Jason Carthen, *52 Ways to Tackle Leadership for Your Success* (Charlotte, NC: I Speak Life, Publishing, 2016), 65.

based work, and focus on collaboration, involves overcoming these individualistic tendencies, and it essentially involves a paradigm shift for many persons and organizations, in determining best approaches and practices for promoting shared goal-setting, clarity of roles, cohesion, and synergy of effort.

Carthen states that "Teams offer the greatest opportunity for synergy, a positive organizational climate, and an immediate increase in productivity."[231] With synergy and collaboration, teams can often address challenging tasks with speed, quality, and sustainability that individuals might not be able to achieve alone.

### *The Importance of Leaders in Developing Teams*

Many of the leadership qualities that result in building effective teams — like building strong relationships, modeling collaboration, mentoring and coaching, and clarifying roles can be seen in effective biblical leaders like Moses with his work with Miriam, Aaron, Joshua, and others, with Nehemiah and the skills he needed to develop a team to rebuild Jerusalem's walls, and with Paul and his work Silas, Timothy, and others.

The distinctions that can be made between team leadership and other forms of leadership can essentially be seen in how the leader relates with those with whom they are leading. Frank Lafasto and Carl Larson's six dimensions of team leadership offer an image of what team leadership looks like.[232] They assert that team leadership: (1) focuses on the goal, (2)

---

[231] Carthen, *52 Ways to Tackle Leadership for Your Success,* 66.
[232] Frank M. J. LaFasto and Carl E. Larson, *When Teams Work Best: 6,000 Team Members and Leaders Tell What It Takes to Succeed* (Thousand Oaks, CA: Sage, 2001), 97-146.

ensures a collaborative climate, (3) builds confidence, (4) demonstrates sufficient technical know-how, (5) sets priorities, and (6) manages performance.

Conversely, leadership that is not team-focused is essentially individualistic in the way it is carried out in an organization. Such leadership is (1) not necessarily focused on a unified goal, but more on individual goals, (2) there is not a climate of collaboration. (3) there aren't inherent behaviors and practices to build confidence among persons through mentoring, coaching, modeling, training, etc., (4) there isn't intentionality around drawing on the expertise of persons to synergize outcomes, and (5) there aren't specific means by which group priorities and performance can be measured.

In terms of the leader's role in developing teams, Greg Stewart, Charles Manz, and Henry Sims, in *Teamwork and Group Dynamics*, offer a continuum of team development where teams move from being externally managed and led to becoming internally managed and led and thus becoming self-led teams.[233] A first step that a leader can take in effectively starting a team, is thus, to begin with the end in mind of helping the team to eventually become self-led. Thus, developing effective teams begins with a leadership approach focused on those who will comprise the team. For the leader, there has to be an initial valuing of teamwork, and belief that the work of a team will be more effective than that of individuals who may be working alone in "silos" within the organization.

Leadership styles are important to team development. Natalia M. Lorinkova, Matthew J. Pearsall, and Henry P. Sims conducted a study that integrates various theories from

---

[233] Greg Stewart, Charles Manz and Henry Sims, *Teamwork and Group Dynamics* (New York: John Wiley and Sons, 1999), 81-107.

leadership and team development literature to resolve ambiguity regarding the relative benefits of empowering and directive leadership styles in teams.[234] Based on longitudinal performance data from 60 teams, their empirical findings suggest that teams led by a directive leader initially outperform those led by an empowering leader, but over time, teams led by empowering leaders experience higher performance improvement because of higher levels of team learning, coordination, empowerment, and mental model development.

While directive leaders may provide clear direction and expectations for their team members to follow, empowering leaders promote autonomy and responsibility. Directive leaders tend to be focused on their viewpoints, experiences, expectations, and vision, and provide leadership by initiating objectives and assigning tasks. On the other hand, empowering leaders enable team members to lead and participate in the decision-making process. Such leaders tend to create an environment that enables followers to work independently.

### *Qualities of Highly Effective Teams*

There is a large degree, then of interdependence, as Stephen Covey posits in the *Seven Habits of Highly Effective People*, that has to be at work for teams in a church/organization to thrive, and this interdependence, as Covey points out, is a

---

[234] Natalie Lorinkova, Matthew J. Pearsall and Henry P. Sims, "Examining the Differential Longitudinal Performance of Directive versus Empowering Leadership in Teams" in *Academy of Management Journal.* 56(2), May 7, 2012.

higher value than *independence*.[235] He states that "Human life is interdependent. We can combine our talents and abilities and create something greater together. Interdependent people combine their efforts with the efforts of others to achieve their greatest success."

According to Patrick Lencioni, several factors can lead to the dysfunction of teams.[236] Lencioni identifies five factors that contribute to team dysfunctions: the absence of trust, fear of conflict, lack of commitment, avoidance of accountability, and inattention to results.

Similarly, Justin Irving identifies six challenges that teams can face:

(1) Being ingrown
(2) Being indecisive
(3) Inaction
(4) Being inefficient
(5) Inequity
(6) Being inconsiderate[237]

While all of these can be limiting factors at any given time, the first major limitation of teams is holding all persons on the team to the same level of accountability and equitably distributing work. Clear expectations need to be established on the front end on what Mark McCloskey and Jim Louwsma in

---

[235] Stephen Covey, *The Seven Habits of Highly Effective People: Powerful Lessons in Personal Change* (New York: Simon and Schuster, 1989), 307-338.

[236] Patrick Lencioni, *The Five Dysfunctions of a Team (A Leadership Parable)* (San Francisco: Jossey-Bass, 2002), Lencioni discusses these five dysfunctions throughout the book.

[237] Justin Irving, (These six principles were discussed in Irving's lecture for ML-924P-30, Teams, Groups and the Transforming Leader, St. Paul, MN: Bethel Theological Seminary, Fall 2020).

*The Art of Virtue-based Transformational Leadership* identify as the 4-Rs — *Relationships, Roles, Responsibilities, and Results.*[238]

Specific antidotes to team dysfunction can be seen in Stephen Kohn and Vincent O'Connell's six essential habits of highly effective teams.[239] They assert that these habits work together, not unlike the members of an effective team. Based on their 50 years of combined organizational development and consulting experience, they assert that highly effective teams generally exhibit the following six habits:

(1) Strengthening emotional capacity to improve team relationships
(2) Expanding team self-awareness
(3) Practicing empathy and respectfulness
(4) Establishing and regulating team norms
(5) Thinking laterally; and
(6) Entrusting team members with appropriate roles.

The essence of a team is that individual entities complement each other.

Why do some teams consistently deliver high performance while other, seemingly identical teams, struggle? This is the question that underlies Alex Pentland's research.[240] He identifies three key communication dynamics that affect

[238] McCloskey and Louwsma, *The Art of Virtue-based Transformational Leadership,* 36-44.
[239] Stephen E. Kohn and Vincent O'Connell, *Six Habits of Highly Effective Teams* (Franklin Lakes, NJ: Career Press, 2008), Kohn and O'Connell elaborate on these six habits throughout the book.
[240] Alex Pentland, "The New Science of Building Great Teams" in *HBR's 10 Must Reads on Teams* (Boston, MA: Harvard Business Review Press, 2013), 1-20.

team performance: energy, engagement, and exploration. He concludes that when teams map their communication behavior over time and then make adjustments that move them closer to the ideal, they can dramatically improve their performance.

High-performing teams can have an impact on moving organizations, including churches, toward higher performance. Effective teams with efficient and competent leaders can work collaboratively to pursue goals and outperform expectations. This is possible when the leader understands their role in building highly effective teams, adjusts their leadership style to the needs of the team, and constructs the context that is most conducive to high performance.

In summary, there are several characteristics of high-performance teams.

(1) They tend to be self-motivated, innovative, and self-led, and produce better outcomes over time than individuals working on the same tasks.

(2) Persons with requisite skills are identified to fulfill particular roles on the team.

(3) They tend to have the right people performing the right roles.

(4) Team members tend to play integral roles in decision-making and achieving team goals.

(5) Leaders foster a supportive environment and a culture that encourages teamwork.

(6) Adequate support for all team members is provided through mentoring, coaching, and training.

(7) There are high levels of commitment to the team's and organization's mission, vision, and purpose.

(8) An atmosphere of relationship-building is fostered.

(9) Collaborative behavior is modeled.

(10) There are means by which team performance is measured in light of mutual accountability.

### *A Case in Point: Epworth Chapel, Baltimore*

An outcome of Epworth Chapel's strategic planning process, *"Epworth 2020"* which was completed and implemented in 2012, was the adoption of the following Mission, Vision, and Purpose (MVP) statement — *"We are a Christ-centered church that seeks to make disciples and transform our community and world through ministries of excellence, effectiveness, and engagement, while engaging in our five core practices of (1) celebrative/passionate worship; (2) relevant fellowship; (3) intentional discipleship; (4) risk-taking mission; and (5) life-changing evangelism."*

Another outcome of *Epworth 2020* was the reorganization of the church's ministries into five ministry teams (based on Acts 2:41-47):

(1) The Worship and Faith Celebration Team

(2) The Discipleship and Faith Development Team

(3) The Fellowship and Faith Connecting Team

(4) The Mission, Outreach, and Faith in Action Team (MOFAT)

(5) The Evangelism and Faith Sharing Team

Each of these ministry teams is led by a team leader (or co-leaders) who has leadership responsibilities for all of the ministries and leaders (ranging from 10 to 15) assigned to that respective ministry area.

Over the past 10 years, we have developed and enacted a process of team leadership development to facilitate church vitality and growth. Over this period, over 50 leaders and potential leaders have participated in team leadership development through seminars, workshops, and individual and group leadership coaching.

This team leadership development process has been aimed at helping leaders across the church:

(1) be clearer about their respective roles, responsibilities, relationships and expected results as leaders,

(2) be clearer about their role as a part of the broader administrative leadership team of the church,

(3) be able to identify where they may be on a spectrum of being transformational versus transactional in their leadership

(4) be able to more effectively coach and equip the leaders and members on their respective teams and ministries in the church.

Over time, we have experienced the development of more effective team leadership and ministry teams across the church, leading to more vital ministry in the church and community. This team leadership approach has opened up avenues among ministry team leaders for intentional collaboration and deeper reflection and inquiry, where participants can better identify their leadership strengths and areas of potential growth as transformational leaders.

*Axiom Six: Develop a Framework and Strategy for Coaching Leaders and Developing a Coaching Culture*

As a certified professional leadership and life coach — through training in two International Coach Federation (ICF) accredited coach training programs, as well as with Harvard University Extension School's Leadership Coaching Strategies program, I have experienced the transformational impact that leadership/life coaching can have on leaders and organizations.

Leadership coaching is typically a one-to-one or perhaps group service for leaders or executives designed to bring about more effective and healthier organizations. Leadership coaching is defined by the International Coach Federation (ICF) as "the process of partnering with clients in a thought-provoking and creative process that inspires them to maximize their personal and professional potential, which is particularly important in today's uncertain and complex environment. Coaches honor the client as the expert in his or her life and work and believe every client is creative, resourceful, and whole.

In defining leadership coaching, the ICF further states that "Hence, when leaders improve their performance, such benefits spread throughout the organization. In a sense, exposing leaders to the coaching experience has a flow-on effect of precipitating a coaching culture within the organization itself. As people responsive to coaching apply their newfound skills and techniques to other people in the organization, the organization then becomes more vital and effective.

Madeline McNeely, lead instructor with Harvard University Extension School's Leadership Coaching Strategies course states that "Coaching is a one-to-one development process between a coach, an organization, and a client, designed to increase the client's leadership and/or managerial performance using feedback processes."[241] Bill Ryan in *Coaching Practices and Prospects Report* points out that over 50% of North American companies (for-profit and non-profit) use coaching.

Leadership coaching begins with the premise that there are already extant leadership qualities that lie within the person who is being coached. Chris Holmes, in *The Art of Coaching Clergy: A Handbook for Church Leaders, Clergy and Coaches,* states that in coaching, "We begin with an individual's amazing resilience, believing each person is capable, wonderfully insightful, gifted, and competent."[242]

Jane Creswell, in *Christ-centered Coaching, Seven Benefits for Ministry,* posits that the seven benefits of Christ-centered coaching are that it (1) leverages strengths, (2) provides clarity and focus, (3) instills confidence, (4) catapults learning, (5) fosters intentional progress, (6) rubs off on others, and (7) encourages God-sized goals.[243]

According to Thomas Hawkins, the critical task of leaders is to multiply leadership through developing the potential of other leaders, and he maintains that coaching

---

[241] Madeline McNeely, "Leadership Coaching Strategies" (Cambridge, MA: Harvard University Extension School, 2019), see course notes.

[242] Chris Holmes, *The Art of Coaching Clergy: A Handbook for Church Leaders, Clergy and Coaches* (Annapolis, MD: Chris Holmes, 2018), xxii.

[243] Jane Creswell, *Christ-centered Coaching: 7 Benefits for Ministry Leaders* (St. Louis, MO: Lake Hickory Resources, 2006), 39-123.

provides both the theory and the tools to develop leaders.[244] Hawkins further posits that coaches are trained to guide others toward greater competence and that effective coaches help persons stay focused on the goals they want to achieve. He proposes that coaching is essentially about the transformation and change of people and organizations.

Typically, leadership coaching falls into one of three categories — *(1) Problem-solving, (2) Feedback, and (3) Developmental.*[245] *Problem-solving coaching* tends to involve solving an issue so that the coachee can progress with new solutions, and involves a good amount of inquiry and advocacy skills. *Feedback coaching* is used when there is a need to interrupt behavior that needs improvement and/or to reinforce behavior/ways of being that the supervisor and/or client want to be replicated and that the work environment requires. Feedback coaching requires using observable data as much as possible to support behavioral change. *Developmental coaching* seeks to enhance skills and align potential with behavior and results. It often involves training and an ongoing process of development and growth for the coachee.

One objective of leadership coaching is to help not only the leader but to improve the effectiveness of the church/organization as a whole. The premise is that when leaders improve their performance, such benefits spread throughout the organization. Another objective of leadership coaching is to help leaders become more aware of their capacity to lead, to identify skills and growing edges in their leadership,

---

[244] Thomas R. Hawkins, *Faithful Guides: Coaching Strategies for Church Leaders* (Nashville, TN: Discipleship Resources, 2006), Hawkins develops his thesis throughout the book.

[245] McNeely, "Leadership Coaching Strategies", see course notes.

and to discover ways that the individual's leadership can serve as a ministry multiplier for developing other transformational leaders.

A template that can be used for leadership coaching is Mark McCloskey and Jim Louwsma's 4-Rs model — where *Relationships, Roles, Responsibilities, and Results* are used as points of inquiry in/for the coaching process. Using this template, a lead question for coaching sessions can be for coaches/participants to state and clarify their general understanding of their *roles, responsibilities, relationships, and results* within the context of their leadership. Follow-up coaching sessions can involve more specific inquiry and discussion as to how the respective leader (coachee) feels that the 4-Rs are playing out in their specific area(s) of leadership. In other words, where can they identify specific strengths and growing edges (challenges) in/with their leadership? Where do they see possibilities for transformation to occur in their leadership and with those whom they are leading?

It could also help, in the coaching process, to use McCloskey and Louwsma's DICE+1 to delve deeper into virtue-based attributes of leadership, and how coaches and the people they are leading are continuing to be transformed through the five aspects of DICE+1 — *Dynamic Determination, Intellectual Flexibility, Courageous Character, Emotional Maturity, and Collaborative Quotient.*[246]

### *A Case in Point: Epworth Chapel, Baltimore*

---

[246] McCloskey and Louwsma, *The Art of Virtue-based Transformational Leadership,* 38-49.

Some of my ongoing leadership development work with leaders at Epworth Chapel over the past 11 years has involved performing individual and group leadership coaching for identified leaders and groups in the churches. As an outcome of Epworth Chapel's strategic planning process in 2011-12 (*Epworth 2020)*, a group of 15 key leaders was selected for coaching based on the key leadership roles and responsibilities that they have in the church, and therefore the expectations that they will model transformational leadership in their ministry areas, among those they are responsible for leading.

A key premise is that developing key leaders is critical to their transformation, and will positively impact their ability to become ministry multipliers and to transform others whom they lead in the church. It is further believed that such development and transformation of leaders through leadership coaching is a key to transforming the church into becoming more vital and effective in its ministries within the church and the broader community.

The objectives of individual and group leadership coaching at Epworth Chapel have been to (1) help each leader be clearer about the difference between transactional and transformational leadership, (2) help each leader identify where they may be on a spectrum of being transformational versus transactional in their leadership, (3) identify how McCloskey and Louwsma's 4-Rs (*Relationships, Roles, Responsibilities and Results*) are at work in their leadership, and (4) be able to coach those with whom they provide leadership in the church.

The impact of leadership coaching at Epworth Chapel over the past 11 years has been that it has been helpful in efforts to strengthen overall leadership in the church. Several coachees (leaders) have shared that leadership coaching has helped them more clearly identify and articulate their roles, relationships, responsibilities, and expected results as leaders. Several have also shared that leadership coaching has helped them develop SMART Goals (specific, measurable, attainable, realistic, and timely) and Ministry Action Plans.

Another positive outcome of the leadership coaching at Epworth has been that it has allowed me as senior pastor and leadership coach to work in intentional one-on-one, and group relationships with key leaders serving in various aspects of church leadership as paid staff and volunteers in administrative and programmatic roles. This one-on-one and group work has helped us continue to strengthen relationships, clarify roles and responsibilities, and intentionally assess results and outcomes, while also serving to help leaders to continue to identify their strengths, gifts, passions, and commitments, and some of their perceived challenges/growing edges.

## *Axiom Seven: Develop a Framework and Strategy for Visioning and Planning*

Vision is defined as a clear view of a desired future state. Many organizations find themselves at the point of myopia. Myopia is the state of being shortsighted or having narrow vision. For organizations, this essentially means adhering to practices, behaviors, habits, values, and fears that result in shortsightedness, narrowness, and the unwillingness to take risks for the sake of a better future. Vision helps people and organizations see how they are moving most fully into their best future.

Michael Crane points out that too often visions are too small. Our visions are sometimes limited to growing our own

148

church or ministry. As a result, churches and ministries become either competitive with or isolated from like-minded organizations. When this happens, Christians become distracted by in-house politicking and tribalism. Church members can become prideful about their own church's growth even though the citywide Christian community is fractured and dysfunctional. Churches and ministries with such limited visions can be a hindrance to what God wants to do in the whole city.[247]

Crane goes on to assert that the beautiful thing about large vision... is that it is impossible to carry out alone.[248] When we engage in a large vision, we are forced to draw on a network of people and resources to accomplish the task.

Three dimensions of vision are (1) *Hindsight* – What has happened in the past?; (2) *Insight* – What is happening in the present?; and (3) *Foresight* – What can be perceived as that which will occur in the future? Lovett Weems offers ten characteristics of vision – (1) A vision is related to the mission but different. (2) A vision is unique. (3) A vision focuses on the future. (4) A vision is for others. (5) A vision is realistic. (6) A vision is lofty. (7) A vision is inviting. (8) A vision is a group vision. (9) A vision is good news and bad news. (10) A vision is a sign of hope.[249]

While working as a consultant on new church development with the United Methodist Church's General Board of Global Ministries several years ago, I was introduced to a visioning process that draws on the agrarian image of

[247] Michael Crane, *Sowing Seeds of Change: Cultivating Change in the City* (Portland, OR: Urban Loft Publishers, 2015), 125.
[248] Crane, *Sowing Seeds of Change*, 126.
[249] Weems, *Church Leadership*, 25-29.

sowing and reaping in 2 Corinthians 9:6-8. This five-part process (identified by the acronym *SOWwithPH: See it. Own it. Work it. Pray it. Help it.*) helps church leaders and stakeholders engage in ministry discernment and implementation. Originally designed to help new church pastors and leaders, I have found the *SOWwithPH* process helpful to those leading churches and religious non-profit organizations through processes of turnaround and revitalization.[250] The following is an outline of the *SOWwithPH* process.

### *1. See It*

"Seeing it" involves vision. Vision is critical to any church/ministry/organization's vitality and growth. From a Christian perspective, vision is the picture of God's preferred future. The late Bishop Rueben P. Job defined vision as "a gift from God. It is the reward of being disciplined, faithful, and patient in listening to God. Vision allows us to see beyond the visible, beyond the barriers and obstacles to our mission. Vision 'catches us up,' captivates and compels us to act."

Lovett Weems intimates that vision shapes our orientation toward reality as well as our sense of being in the world. It is the gift of eyes of faith to see the invisible, to know the unknowable, to think the unthinkable, and to experience the "not yet." It is our vision that draws us forward.[251]

### *2. Own It*

---

[250] C. Anthony Hunt, "5 Steps to Church Vitality and Turnaround" in *Leading Ideas*, (Washington, DC: Lewis Center for Church Leadership, October 11, 2017.
[251] Weems, *Church Leadership*, 26.

"Owning it" speaks to the way that vision is shared across the organization, and with other stakeholders. It also speaks to an awareness of the current realities of the church or organization in light of its hopes for the future. Leaders and stakeholders can use tools such as ministry charting, community or church diagnostics, demographic data such as U.S. Census and MissionInsite data, asset mapping, community assessments, and ministry-by-walking-around (MBWA) - to help in the processes of ministry ownership, community buy-in, and developing partnerships.

### 3. Work It

"Working it" speaks to ways that ministry is activated and implemented. It is ministry in action. This should be aligned with the stated mission, vision, and purpose (MVP) of the church or ministry and should include strategies for marketing, community engagement, outreach and evangelism, use of social media and technology, and creative programming including - worship, Christian Education, small group ministries, mission and outreach, and community engagement.

### 4. Pray It

"Praying it" involves the use of spiritual disciplines and spiritual formation in the process of ongoing ministry discernment and implementation. Intentionally encouraging leaders and stakeholders to practice inward, outward, and corporate spiritual disciplines and then celebrating the visible impact of ministry in the lives of people moves the church towards greater vitality. At Epworth Chapel, we have found Richard Foster's book, *Celebration of Discipline*, to be a helpful spiritual resource in our ongoing turnaround efforts as we continue to pray for our mission, vision, and purpose.

## 5. Help It

To actualize, sustain, and grow a vision, it is critical to discern what help is needed at various stages in a church's lifecycle. "Helping it" involves determining what denominational and community support, consultants, coaches, technical assistance, and resources are needed to continue to move the mission, vision, and purpose forward.

Engaging in a process like *SOWwithPH* can be helpful to churches that are seeking to discern and implement a mission, vision, and purpose over the life cycle of their ministry. By using the *SOWwithPH* process as a vision and planning resource, Epworth Chapel has been able to clarify its mission, vision, and purpose, with a shared commitment to continuing to work through the various phases of the *SOWwithPH* process.

## A Case in Point: Epworth Chapel, Baltimore

Shortly after I was appointed pastor of Epworth Chapel United Methodist Church in Baltimore in 2011, the Church Council began a visioning process to discern God's vision and ministry plan for the church. Information gleaned from MissionInsite data about the current and projected demographic makeup in our zip code, and the use of the *SOWwithPH* process helped us clarify our mission, vision, and purpose, and helped us enact our stated mission – *"to make disciples of Jesus Christ and make a difference for the transformation for our community and the world."*

We developed a strategic plan, *"Epworth 2020,"* that included an organizational restructuring which led to the formation of five ministry teams as stated earlier in this volume. To help continue to move the mission and vision forward, Epworth Chapel holds an annual churchwide Leadership, Vision, and Planning retreat, facilitated by denominational consultants, that has been designed to build leadership capacity around issues like community change, multicultural competence, stewardship development, ministry outside the church wall, effective team building, and turning vision into action.

A key learning for us is that visioning and planning are ongoing processes. They are processes that must be intentional, focused, and consistent, and there must be internal means of assessment and evaluation of the church's and leader's effectiveness in visioning and planning over time.

## *A Case in Point: Metropolitan Baptist Church, Washington, DC*

In *On Jordan's Stormy Banks: Leading Your Congregation through the Wilderness of Change,* H. Beecher Hicks asserts that the ability of leaders to cast vision is essential for leading churches through change. He states that a clear vision statement is necessary because it helps both the pastor and church understand where the ministry is going, how it is going to get there, and what desired outcomes and expectations are once it has arrived. Vision is vital for ministry. Without vision, people cannot see or grasp their direction.[252]

---

[252] H. Beecher Hicks, Jr., *On Jordan's Stormy Banks: Leading Your Congregation through the Wilderness of Change,* (Grand Rapids, MI: Zondervan, 2004), 10.

Based on his research and 34 years of experience as the pastor of Metropolitan Baptist Church in Washington, DC, Hicks outlines twelve principles for visionary leadership.[253] These principles are:

(1) Proper planning is essential for effective visioning and vision implementation.

(2) Keep the people informed.

(3) The leader is central to the vision-casting and buy-in process.

(4) The congregation sees the person before they see the vision.

(5) Competing voices within the church make it difficult for the congregation to hear what is truly being said, no matter how precise the language is.

(6) It will be difficult for the congregation to conceptualize the vision.

(7) Vision-casting implies customized change.

(8) The visionary must avoid distractions.

(9) Vision-casting takes time.

(10) The congregation has a responsibility.

(11) "Everybody Talkin' 'bout Heaven Ain't Goin' There!".

(12) The Struggle Will Continue.

Lovett Weems states that leadership is the ability to anticipate the future based on the past and present. One description of the leader says, "Our leaders tell us what we are thinking. Our leaders tell us what we are feeling." When true

---

[253] Hicks, *On Jordan's Stormy Banks,* 215-226.

visions emerge, the response of the people in the group is a nod of recognition, identification, and affirmation.[254] Importantly, transformational leaders essentially become the chief visionaries of their organization and must be able to clearly and consistently communicate the need for change in compelling and convincing ways and then draw others into the process of facilitating and implementing change.

## *Conclusion*

There is hope for the city! *In The Leading Causes of Life*, Gary Gunderson and Larry Pray assert that hope is a leading cause of life. They state that hope is tied to that to which we are most connected. In times of "frightful transition", we are to call out those who come to steal our hope.[255]

In a 1967 sermon, "The Meaning of Hope," Martin Luther King, Jr. defined hope as that quality that is "necessary for life."[256] He asserted that hope was to be viewed as "animated and undergirded by faith and love." In his mind, if you have hope, you have faith in something. Thus, hope shares the belief that "all reality hinges on moral foundations."[257] Hope beckons us to act.

A clarion call for churches is to act in developing transformed transformational leaders who will help move

---

[254] Weems, *Church Leadership*, 42.
[255] Gary Gunderson and Larry Pray, *The Leading Causes of Life* (Nashville: Abingdon, 2009), 137.
[256] Martin Luther King, Jr., "The Meaning of Hope," sermon delivered on December 10, 1967; Martin Luther King, Jr. King Center Archives, Atlanta, GA, 5ff.
[257] King, "The Meaning of Hope".

people and organizations toward realizing God's preferred future. Given the unique challenges and great opportunities facing urban churches and communities today, a critical task is to devise processes and frameworks for developing transformational leaders who can serve in unique urban ministry settings.

In concluding this volume, the story of the two little brothers comes to mind. The boys couldn't stay out of trouble (anything they could get into, they got into). Their parents – frustrated that they could not get the brothers to behave – decided to take them to see the pastor of their church. The pastor had the younger of the two boys come into the office first, and began to query him, "Tell me, where is God...?", he asked the boy several times, "Where is God...?" The boy, now frightened, got up and took off running to his house, and went up to his bedroom and hid in the closet. His big brother followed him home and found him in the closet, and asked him what had happened to make him so afraid. The little boy said, "I'm not sure, but God is missing, and the pastor thinks that you and I stole God."

In a world fraught with political, social, and economic upheaval, many people today are asking, "where is God?" And it is a part of the vocation of transformational church, religious, and nonprofit leaders to help people in churches, institutions, and communities locate God.

Indeed, God is calling churches to prepare transformational leaders and this must start by understanding the specific mission God has for churches in their respective communities. Connected with their vision and mission, God calls churches to have a clear sense of how they will engage in calling, equipping, and supporting transformational leaders to serve the church and its community.

In this regard, the church is called to be consistently introspective and reflective on exactly who it is, and where it is, and then determine where God is leading it into the future. The church and community must be willing to meet at the intersections of healing and hope - especially in urban ministry contexts, and the church must see itself in every person it encounters and work together in the community until transformation occurs.

In this volume, I have sought to address the need for transformational leadership development for persons serving in urban ministry settings and to offer seven axioms that could serve as foundations for shaping contextualized processes and models for transformational leadership development in such settings.

I hope that this volume will serve as a framework for well-developed, sustainable, scalable transformational leadership development processes and models for persons serving in the leadership in urban ministry settings.

My ultimate hope is that this will help churches and their leaders fully connect with their communities and that it will serve as a resource for churches to be intentional about developing transformational leaders who are called, convicted, connected, and committed to courageously helping bring about transformation, vitality, and flourishing in urban churches and communities.

There is hope for the city!! The prophet Jeremiah's words of hope ring as true today as they did 2600 years ago, "*I know the plans I have for you, says the Lord, plans to prosper*

*you, and not harm you, plans to give you a future with hope."*
May it be so.

## *EPILOGUE I - GOT HOPE! (A SERMON)*

*Therefore, since we have been justified through faith, we have peace with God through our Lord Jesus Christ, through whom we have gained access by faith into this grace in which we now stand. And we boast in the hope of the glory of God. Not only so, but we also glory in our sufferings because we know that suffering produces perseverance; perseverance, character; and character, hope. And hope does not put us to shame, because God's love has been poured out into our hearts through the Holy Spirit, who has been given to us.*
*(Romans 5:1-5)*

*(This sermon was first delivered at Epworth Chapel UMC, Baltimore, MD in April 2015 in the aftermath of the police-involved death of Freddie Gray, and then delivered as the keynote address at the international meeting of the Association of United Methodist Chancellors in Baltimore, MD in May 2015.)*

This week has been filled with tumult and turmoil just in our backyard. We have experienced the very public funeral of Mr. Freddie Gray here in Baltimore, in the aftermath of his police-involved death. We've witnessed the lashing out of many of our young people — and some who are not so young — who have expressed their frustration and outrage by rioting and looting at Mondawmin Mall — just a few miles from where we sit today.

We've witnessed the destruction of several drug stores, food markets, and other places of business, and the destruction and burning of houses, cars, and church property across the city.

We've witnessed lashing out with violence against police officers. We've seen the military presence of the Maryland National Guard planted in the city to maintain order on Baltimore's streets.

We've experienced a city-wide curfew, and we've witnessed numerous people being arrested. And amidst all of this, there were at least five more people murdered in Baltimore, and at least 12 more shot in the past week — one of those murdered being a close friend of the late Freddie Gray. We've seen local and state officials wrestle with what would be the best course of action to bring about peace and justice for Mr. Gray's family, the Sandtown-Winchester community, zip code 21217, and the city of Baltimore.

The eyes of the entire nation and world have been turned to Baltimore. We've seen and experienced what has appeared to be hopelessness, and what can happen when some people among us feel hopeless, invisible, and unheard. Martin Luther King, Jr. intimated that "riots are the language of the unheard."

And amidst all of this turmoil — we have also seen many people come together to pray for peace and justice in Baltimore. We've seen people gather to march in peaceful protest. We've seen people come together to work to rebuild communities across Baltimore, a city torn by decades of destruction and neglect. We've seen churches open their doors to feed the hungry and provide a haven for children. We've seen some people celebrate at the announcement that criminal charges would be brought against the six police officers involved in Mr. Gray's death.

We have witnessed members of the Baltimore Symphony Orchestra leave their music halls amid the rioting to offer beautiful music on the city's streets. We've seen phenomenal acts of generosity and kindness. So, in the midst of all that we've gone through this past week – through it all — we realize that we've still got hope.

The days, times, and conditions in which the apostle Paul ministered were probably in many ways similar to what we are experiencing today. In Rome, there was, at points, an apparent paucity of hope — even among people who had come to know of the living Christ. Paul was preaching to this apparent paucity of hope. Maybe this was due to the existence of severe persecution of the people in the church because they believed in Christ, or maybe it was because of the very real challenges that they faced in their daily lives.

In many ways, the church today is well-acquainted with the realities, both within and outside the church, that challenge our hopefulness. Indeed, a look at the world and the church today gives a clear indication that we teeter on the brink of hopelessness and despair — with wars that have lasted too long and killed too many, violence in too many of our neighborhoods, increasing gaps between the "have-gots" and the "have-nots", political discord, and the inordinate number of matters that threaten to divide the churches and our communities. We teeter on the brink of hopelessness.

And yet, if the church has been, and is to be anything, we are to be a people who boldly embodies hope. This was Paul's point in his words to Christians in Rome:

> *"...and we boast in our hope of sharing the glory of God... knowing that our suffering produces endurance, and endurance produces character, and character produces hope, and hope does not disappoint us..."*
> *(Roams 5:3)*

Hope is real and should be real to you and me. Hope is what German theologian Jurgen Moltmann wrote about in *A Theology of Hope* when he intimated –

> *Hope alone is to be called "realistic" because it alone takes seriously the possibilities with which all reality is fraught. Hope does not take things as they happen to stand or to lie, but as progressing, moving things with possibilities of change.*[258]

Hope assures us that justice will come... peace will come.... and that change is going to come.

We've got hope! One of the things I've learned about hope is that there are times when we tend to trivialize and even mythicize hope so much so that we often don't recognize it even when it is in our midst. But if we take the time to look carefully, we will see hope all around us.

Children laughing and playing, that's hope. Music in our ears, that's hope. Food on our tables, that's hope. Clothes on our backs, that's hope. Shoes on our feet, that's hope. Shelter over our heads, that's hope. New awakenings and new beginnings, that's hope!

And so, whatever our lot today and whatever the future holds for us, as people in and of Christ, we've got hope! And let us be reminded of where our hope is rooted. Our hope is in the name of Jesus.

Hope lets us wake up knowing that *"morning by morning new mercies (we) see"* (Lamentations 3:23). Hope lets us lie down at night knowing that *"weeping may endure for a night, but joy comes in the morning"* (Psalm 30:5). Hope

---

[258] Jurgen Moltmann, *Theology of Hope* (Louisville, KY: Westminster John Knox, 1978), 25.

reminds us that *"faith is the substance of things hoped for, and the evidence of things not seen"* (Hebrews 11:1). Hope is what the song-writer knew of when she wrote -

*Time is filled with swift transitions.*
*Naught of earth unmoved can stand.*
*Build your hopes on things eternal.*
*Hold to God's unchanging hand.*

*Hold to God's hand, God's unchanging hand.*
*Hold to God's hand, God's unchanging hand.*
*Build your hopes on things eternal.*
*Hold to God's unchanging hand.*
*(Hold to God's Unchanging Hand)*
(Jennie Wilson)

We've Got Hope!

# EPILOGUE II - A PRAYER FOR CITIES

God, "you're the God of this city. You're the King of these people. You're the Lord of the nation. You are… You're the light in this darkness. You're the hope to the hopeless. You're the peace to the restless. You are." (Chris Tomlin)

O God, you see all and know all — and amidst the various vicissitudes of life, we are mindful that you are in control of all that is and is to be. We thank you for your grace and mercy toward us. We are a people of divergent perspectives, with a diversity of hopes, dreams, and visions. But we come before you acknowledging the commonality that all persons share in you, the creator of the universe.

We offer you thanks for cities across America and the world, and we take this opportunity to offer prayers for each city. We pray that you will bless every home and every community — every school and every place where your people gather for work and leisure. Bless those persons who are older and those who are younger. We pray for peace and safety for all people who live and move throughout every community across the nation, and we pray likewise for communities like ours around the world.

Lord God, we pray especially for your blessings to be with those persons who bear the burdens of want and disparity among us — whether it be for lack of food or shelter, inadequate healthcare, or inadequate education.

We ask for your blessings on those who serve and lead our cities in elective and appointive office, and those who will do so in the future. Bless them with a portion of your wisdom, patience, integrity, justice, and compassion. We pray for churches and other religious and community institutions that seek to promote good and provide for the spiritual, material, and social well-being of your people.

We pray that we would realize the promise that God made through the prophet Jeremiah that God has a future filled with hope in store for each of us.

Indeed, "you're the God of this city. You're the King of these people. You're the Lord of the nation. You are... You're the light in this darkness. You're the hope to the hopeless. You're the peace to the restless. You are." (Chris Tomlin)

# BIBLIOGRAPHY

Bakke, Ray and Jim Hart. *The Urban Christian: Effective Ministry in Today's Urban World.* Downers Grove, IL: InterVarsity Press, 1987.

Bartman, John and John Muddiman, eds. *Oxford Bible Commentary.* Oxford, UK: Oxford University Press, 2001.

Becker, Jurgen. *Paul: The Apostle to the Gentiles.* trans. O. C. Dean, Jr. Louisville: Westminster John Knox, 1993.

Bennis, Warren, and Robert Thomas, "The Crucibles of Leadership," in *HBR's 10 Must Reads on Leadership.* Boston, MA: Harvard Business Review Press, 2011.

Blount, Brian, ed. *True to Our Native Land: An African American New Testament Commentary.* Minneapolis, MN: Fortress Press, 2007.

Bobo, Kimberly. "Church Involvement in Community Organizations." *Review & Expositor* 92, no. 1 (February 1995): 31–38, accessed August 28, 2022.

Bolman, Lee G. and Terrance Deal. *Reframing Organizations: Artistry, Choice, and Leadership*, 6th ed. San Francisco: Jossey-Bass, 2017.

Bonhoeffer, Dietrich. *Life Together: The Classic Exploration of Faith in Community.* trans. John Doberstein. New York: Harper Collins, 1954.

Bordas, Juana. *Salsa, Soul, and Spirit: Leadership for a Multicultural Age: New Approaches to Leadership from Latino, Black, and American Indian Communities,* 2nd ed. (San Francisco, CA: Berrett-Koehler, 2012.

Borg, Marcus J. and John Dominic Crossan. *The First Paul: Reclaiming the Radical The Visionary Behind the Church's Conservative Icon.* New York: HarperCollins, 2009.

Bowens, Lisa M. *African American Readings of Paul: Reception, Resistance, and Transformation.* Grand Rapids, MI: William B. Eerdmans, 2020.

Boyarin, Daniel. *A Radical Jew: Paul and the Politics of Identity.* Berkley: University of California Press, 1994.

Braxton, Brad. *Preaching Paul.* Nashville, TN: Abingdon Press, 2004.

Breneman, Mervin. *The New American Commentary: An Exegetical and Theological Exposition of Holy Scripture (Ezra, Nehemiah, Esther).* Nashville, TN: Broadman and Holman Publishers, 1993.

Brown, Lawrence T. *The Black Butterfly: The Harmful Politics of Race and Space in America.* Baltimore, MD: Johns Hopkins University Press, 2021.

_____. "Two Baltimores: The White L vs. the Black Butterfly," *Baltimore Sun,* June 28, 2016.

Brown, Olu. *Leadership Directions from Moses: On the Way to a Promised Land.* Nashville, TN: Abingdon Press, 2017.

Brown, Raymond. *The Bible Speaks Today: The Message of Nehemiah.* Downers Grove, IL: Intervarsity Press, 1998.

Brueggemann, Walter. *A Gospel of Hope.* Louisville, KY: Westminster John Knox Press, 2018.

Bugg, Charles B. *Transformational Leadership: Leading with Integrity.* Macon, GA: Smyth and Helwys Publishers, 2010.

Burns, James Macgregor. *Transforming Leadership.* New York: Grove Press, 2004.

Byassee, Jason. "Strategies for Urban Ministry", *The Christian Century*, March 8, 2008.

Carle, Robert D., and Louis A. DeCaro, Jr., eds. *Signs of Hope in the City: Ministries of Community Renewal.* Valley Forge, PA: Judson Press, 1999.

Carthen, Jason. *52 Ways to Tackle Leadership for Your Success.* Charlotte, NC: I Speak Life, Publishing, 2016.

Chudacoff, Howard P. and Judith E. Smith. *The Evolution of the American Urban Society* Edgewood Cliff, NJ: Prentice Hall Press, 1988.

Cladis, George. *Leading the Team-Based Church.* San Francisco, CA: Jossey-Bass Publishers, 1999.

Claerbaut, David. *Urban Ministry in a New Millennium.* Federal Way, WA: World Vision, 2005.

Collins, Jim and Morten Hansen. *Great by Choice: Chaos, Uncertainty, and Luck.* New York: Harper Collins, 2011.

Conn, Harvie M. and Daniel Ortiz. *Urban Ministry: The Kingdom of God, the City, and the People of God.* Downers Grove, IL: InterVarsity Press, 2001.

Covey, Stephen. *The Seven Habits of Highly Effective People: Powerful Lessons in Personal Change.* New York: Simon and Schuster, 1989.

Cox, Harvey Gallagher. *The Secular City: Secularization and Urbanization in Theological Perspective.* New York: MacMillan, 1966.

Crane, Michael. *Sowing Seeds of Change: Cultivating Change in the City.* Portland, OR: Urban Loft Publishers, 2015.

Creswell, Jane. *Christ-centered Coaching: 7 Benefits for Ministry Leaders.* St. Louis, MO: Lake Hickory Resources, 2006.

Daniels, Joseph. *Walking with Nehemiah: Your Community is Your Congregation.* Nashville: Abingdon Press, 2014.

Dayton, Edward R. and Ted Engstrom. *Strategy for Leadership: Planning, Activating, Motivating, Elevating.* Grand Rapids, MI: Fleming H. Revell, 1979.

Easum, Bill. *Unfreezing Moves: Following Jesus into the Mission Field*. Nashville: Abingdon Press, 2002.

Egan, Harvey D. *Christian Mysticism: The Future of a Tradition*. New York: Pueblo Publishing, 1984.

Euchner, Charles and Stephen McGovern. *Urban Policy Reconsidered: Dialogues on the Problems and Prospects of American Cities*. New York: Routledge, 2003.

Foster, Lionel. "The Black Butterfly: Racial Segregation and Investment Patterns in Baltimore" in *Urban Institute*. Washington, DC: Urban Institute, February 5, 2019.

Francis, Leah Gunning. *Faith after Ferguson: Resilient Leadership in Pursuit of Racial Justice*. St. Louis, MO: Chalice Press, 2021.

_____. *Ferguson and Faith: Sparking Leadership and Awakening Community*. St. Louis, MO: Chalice Press, 2015.

Francis, Pope. *The Joy of the Gospel (Evangelii Gaudium)*. Washington, DC: U.S. Office of Catholic Bishops, 2007.

_____. Francis, Pope. *Laudato Si – Encyclical Letter*. Vatican City: Liberia Elditrice Vaticana, June 18, 2015.

Franklin, Robert M. *Crisis in the Village: Restoring Hope in African American Communities*. Minneapolis, Fortress Press, 2007.

Gench, Roger J. *Theology from the Trenches: Reflections on Urban Ministry*. Louisville: Westminster John Knox Press, 2014.

Gorman, Michael J. *Reading Paul*. Eugene, OR: Cascade Books, 2008.

Gornik, Mark R. *To Live in Peace: Biblical Faith and the Changing Inner City*. Grand Rapids, MI: Eerdmans, 2002.

Gunderson, Gary and Larry Pray. *The Leading Causes of Life.* Nashville, TN: Abingdon, 2009.

Hamilton, James M. *Christian-centered Exposition: Exalting Jesus in Ezra and Nehemiah.* Nashville, TN: Holman Reference, 2014.

Harper, Nile. *Urban Churches: Vital Signs - Beyond Charity, Toward Justice.* Grand Rapids: Eerdmans Publishing, 1999.

Harrington, Daniel and James Keenan. *Paul and Virtue Ethics. Lanham, MD: Rowman and Littlefield Publishers, 2010.*

Hawkins, Thomas R. *Faithful Guides: Coaching Strategies for Church Leaders.* Nashville, TN: Discipleship Resources, 2006.

Heifetz, Ronald, Alexander Grashow, and Marty Linsky. *The Practice of Adaptive Leadership: Tools and Tactics for Changing Your Organization and the World.* Boston, MA: Harvard Business Press, 2009.

Hicks, H. Beecher. *On Jordon's Stormy Banks: Leading Your Congregation through the Wilderness of Change.* Grand Rapids: Zondervan, 2004.

Hill, Craig C. "Romans" in *The Oxford Bible Commentary.* John Bartman, and John Muddiman, eds. Oxford, UK: Oxford University Press, 2001.

Holman, Frederick C. *Ezra and Nehemiah: Israel Alive Again (International Theological Commentary).* Grand Rapids, MI: Eerdmans, 1987.

Holmes, Chris. *The Art of Coaching Clergy: A Handbook for Church Leaders, Clergy and Coaches.* Annapolis, MD: Chris Holmes, 2018.

Horsely, Richard A. "1 Corinthians: A Case Study of Paul's Assembly as an Alternative World" in *Paul and Empire:*

*Religions and Power in Roman Imperial Society,* Richard Horsley, ed. Harrisburg, PA: Trinity Press International, 1997.

Hunt, C. Anthony. "5 Steps to Church Vitality and Turnaround" in *Leading Ideas.* Washington, DC: Lewis Center for Church Leadership, October 11, 2017.

_____. "Three Keys to Identify and Develop High Impact Leaders" in *Leading Ideas.* Washington, DC: Lewis Center for Church Leadership, May 18, 2016.

_____. "Why the Church's Mission Really Matters in this Time of Crisis" in *Leading Ideas.* Washington, DC: Lewis Center for Church Leadership, June 3, 2020.

Irving, Justin. "Decentralization and the Shared Leadership of the New Testament", 2004. Paper presented in ML-924P-30, Teams, Groups and the Transforming Leader, Bethel Theological Seminary, St. Paul, MN, Spring, 2021.

Jacobsen, Dennis A. *Doing Justice: Congregations and Community Organizing.* Minneapolis: Fortress Press, 2001.

Katzenbach, Jon R. and Douglas K. Smith. "The Discipline of Teams", *HBR's 10 Must Reads on Teams.* Boston, MA: Harvard Business Review Press, 2013.

Keener, Craig S. *The IVP Bible Background Commentary, New Testament.* Downers Grove, IL: InterVarsity Press, 1993.

King, Martin Luther, Jr., "The Meaning of Hope". Atlanta, GA: Martin Luther King, Jr. King Center Archives. The sermon was delivered on December 10, 1967.

_____. *Strength to Love.* Philadelphia, PA: Fortress Press, 1963.

King, Ursula. *Christian Mystics: Their Lives and Legacies Throughout the Ages.* Mahwah, NJ: Hidden Spring, 2001.

Kohn, Stephen E. and Vincent O'Connell, *Six Habits of Highly Effective Teams.* Franklin Lakes, NJ: Career Press, 2008.

Kotter, John P. *Leading Change.* Boston, MA: Harvard Business School, 1996.

_____. *What Leaders Really Do.* Cambridge, MA: Harvard Business Review Book, 1999.

_____. "What Leaders Really Do", in *HBR's 10 Must Reads on Leadership.* Boston, MA: Harvard Business Review Press, 2011.

Lacugna, Catherine. *God for Us: The Trinity and Christian Life.* (San Francisco: HarperCollins, 1973.

LaFasto, Frank M. J. and Carl E. Larson. *When Teams Work Best: 6,000 Team Members and Leaders Tell What It Takes to Succeed.* Thousand Oaks, CA: Sage, 2001.

Lencioni, Patrick. *The Five Dysfunctions of a Team (A Leadership Parable).* San Francisco: Jossey-Bass, 2002.

Lewin, Kurt. *Field Theory in Social Science.* New York: Harper and Row, 1947.

Lewis, Candace M., and Rodney Thomas Smothers, *Resurgence: Navigating the Changing Ministry Landscape.* Nashville, TN: Heritage Publishing, 2018.

Linthicum, Robert. *Building a People of Power, Equipping Churches to Transform their Communities.* Federal Way, WA: World Vision, 2005.

Lorinkova, Natalie M., Matthew J. Pearsall, and Henry P. Sims, "Examining the Differential Longitudinal Performance of Directive versus Empowering

Leadership in Teams" in *Academy of Management Journal.* 56(2), May 7, 2012

Lupton, Robert. *Toxic Charity: How Churches and Charities Hurt Those They Help.* San Francisco, HarperOne, 2011.

Marbury, Herbert. "Ezra and Nehemiah" in *The Africana Bible: Reading Israel's Scriptures from Africa and the African Diaspora,* Hugh R. Page, Jr. ed. Minneapolis: Fortress Press, 2010.

Mays, James L., ed. *Harper's Bible Commentary.* New York: Harper Collins, 1988.

McCloskey, Mark and Jim Louwsma. *The Art of Virtue-Based Transformational Leadership: Building Strong Businesses, Organizations, and Families.* Bloomington, MN: The Wordsmith, 2014.

McKenzie, Vashti M. *Not Without a Struggle: Leadership Development for African American Women in Ministry.* Cleveland, OH: United Church Press, 1996.

Metzger, Bruce and Michael Coogan, eds. *The Oxford Companion to the Bible.* Oxford, UK: Oxford University Press, 1993.

Northouse, Peter. *Leadership: Theory and Practice, 8th edition.* Los Angeles: Sage Publications, Inc., 2019.

Nouwen Henri J.M. *In the Name of Jesus: Reflections on Christian Leadership.* New York: The Crossroad Publishing Company. 2002.

_____. *The Selfless Way of Christ: Downward Mobility and the Spiritual Life.* New York: Orbis, 2007.

Pentland, Alex. "The New Science of Building Great Teams" in *HBR's 10 Must Reads on Teams.* Boston, MA: Harvard Business Review Press, 2013.

Perkins, John M. *Beyond Charity: A Community Development Handbook for Christians.* Grand Rapids, MI: Baker Book House, 1993.

Perkins, John M., ed. *Restoring At-Risk Communities: Doing It Together and Doing It Right.* Grand Rapids, MI: Baker Books, 1995.

Peters, Ronald E. *Urban Ministry: An Introduction.* Nashville: Abingdon Press, 2007.

Peterson, Eugene. *The Message: The Bible in Contemporary Language.* Colorado Springs, CO: NavPress, 2003.

_____. *Traveling Light: Modern Meditations on Paul's Letter of Freedom.* Colorado Springs, CO: Helmers and Howard, 1988.

Phillips, Katie Carson. "6 Leadership Practices to Enhance Involvement and Collaboration" in *Leading Ideas.* Washington, DC, Lewis Center for Church Leadership, March 2020).

Pretter, Donna and Thomas Pretter. *Nehemiah: NIV Application Commentary.* Grand Rapids, MI: Zondervan, 2020.

Quinn, Robert. *Building the Bridge as You Walk on It: Guide to Leading Change.* San Francisco; Jossey-Bass, 2004.

Rasmus, Rudy. "Leading Ministry with the Homeless", in *Leading Ideas.* Washington, DC: Lewis Center for Church Leadership, June 24, 2009.

Reid, Frank Madison III. *The Nehemiah Plan: Preparing the Church to Rebuild Broken Lives.* Shippensburg, PA: Treasure House, 1993.

Sanders, E. P. *Paul: Very Short Introduction* (Oxford, UK: Oxford University Press, 1991.

Schreiner, Thomas R. *Interpreting the Pauline Epistles.* Grand Rapids, MI: Baker Book House, 1990.

Simon, Nina. *Art of Relevance.* Santa Cruz, CA: Museum Publishing, 2016.

Skjegstad, Joy F. *7 Creative Models for Community Ministry.* Valley Forge, PA: Judson Press, 2013.

St. Ambrose, Bishop of Milan. *Commentary of St. Ambrose on the Gospel according to St. Luke, V.* Dublin, Ireland: Halcyon Press, 2001.

St. Augustine of Hippo, *De morribus eccl.*, Chapter XV in *Nicene and Post-Nicene Fathers*, First Series, Vol. 4, ed. Phillip Schaff (Buffalo, NY: Christian Literature Publishing Co., 1987.

Stewart, Carlyle Fielding, III. *The Empowerment Church: Speaking a New Language for Church Growth.* Nashville: Abingdon Press, 2001.

Stewart, Greg, Charles Manz, and Henry Sims. *Teamwork and Group Dynamics.* New York: John Wiley and Sons, 1999.

Stone, Bryan P. and Claire E. Wolfteich. *Sabbath in the City: Sustaining Urban Pastoral Excellence.* Louisville, KY: Westminster John Knox Press, 2008.*The Holy Bible*, New International Version. Colorado Springs, CO: International Bible Society, 1984.

Throntveit, Mark. *Ezra-Nehemiah: Interpretation - A Bible Commentary for Teaching and Preaching.* Louisville, KY: Westminster John Knox Press, 1992.

Tonna, Benjamin. *Gospel for the Cities: A Socio-Theology of Urban Ministry.* Maryknoll, NY: Orbis Books, 1985.

Venable-Ridley, C. Michelle. "Paul and the African American Community" in *Embracing the Spirit: Womanist*

*Perspectives on Hope, Salvation, and Transformation,* ed. Emilie M. Townes. Maryknoll, NY: Orbis, 1997.

Villafane, Eldin, Bruce Jackson, Robert Evans, Alice Frazier, eds. *Transforming the City: Reframing Education for Urban Ministry* (Grand Rapids, MI: Eerdmans, 2001.

Vyhmeister, Nancy Jean. *Quality Research Papers.* Grand Rapids, MI: Zondervan, 2008.

Weems, Lovett, H., Jr. *Church Leadership: Vision, Culture, Team, and Integrity.* Nashville, TN: Abingdon, 2010.

_____. *Take the Next Step: Leading Lasting Change in the Church.* Nashville, TN: Abingdon, 2003.

Willimon, William. *Pastor: The Theology and Practice of Ordained Ministry.* Nashville, TN: Abingdon Press, 2002.

Wilson, William Julius. *More than Just Race: Being Black and Poor in the Inner City.* New York: W. W. Norton, 2009.

Wright, N. T. *Paul: A Biography.* San Francisco: HarperCollins, 2011.

Yamauchi, Edwin. "Nehemiah" in *The Expositor's Bible Commentary: Volume 4.* ed. Frank E. Gaebelein, Grand Rapids, MI: Zondervan, 1988.

## ABOUT THE AUTHOR

A native of Washington D.C., Rev. Dr. C. Anthony Hunt is the Senior Pastor of Epworth Chapel United Methodist Church in Baltimore, MD, and Professor of Systematic, Moral, and Practical Theology and Permanent Dunning Distinguished Lecturer at the Ecumenical Institute of Theology, St. Mary's Seminary and University in Baltimore. He also teaches at Wesley Theological Seminary in Washington, DC, United Theological Seminary in Dayton, OH, and the Graduate Theological Foundation in Oklahoma City, OK, where he is a Faculty Fellow and E. Franklin Frazier Professor of African-American Studies.

A graduate of the University of Maryland, he holds advanced degrees from Troy University, Wesley Theological Seminary, and the Graduate Theological Foundation. Additionally, he has completed post-graduate studies at the Said Business School at the University of Oxford, UK; Bethel University, St. Paul, MN; St. Mary's Seminary and University, Baltimore, MD; the Center of Theological Inquiry, Princeton, NJ; Harvard University, and the Institute of Certified Professional Managers, James Madison University, Harrisonburg, Va. He is an inductee in the Martin Luther King, Jr. Board of Preachers at Morehouse College, Atlanta, GA.

Dr. Hunt is the author of fifteen other books including *Things that Matter: Messages for Transformed Living* (2022); *Hope Sings: Sermons on the Psalms, Volume 3* (2021); *Holding onto Hope: Essays, Sermons and Prayers on Religion and Race, Volume 4* (2020); *Songs for the Seasons: Sermons on the Psalms, Volume 2* (2020); *I've seen the Promised Land: Martin Luther King, Jr. and the 21ˢᵗ-Century Quest for the Beloved*

*Community* (2020); and *Come Go with Me: Howard Thurman and a Gospel of Radical Inclusivity* (2019), and over 200 articles, chapters and academic papers on matters about religion and society.

Made in the USA
Middletown, DE
18 November 2025

22174221R00099